V&R Academic

Passages – Transitions – Intersections

Volume 3

General Editors:
Paola Partenza (University of Chieti-Pescara, Italy)
Andrea Mariani (University of Chieti-Pescara, Italy)

Advisory Board:
Gianfranca Balestra (University of Siena, Italy)
Barbara M. Benedict (Trinity College Connecticut, USA)
Gert Buelens (University of Ghent, Belgium)
Jennifer Kilgore-Caradec (University of Caen, and ICP, France)
Esra Melikoglu (University of Istanbul, Turkey)
Michal Peprník (University of Olomouc, Czech Republic)
John Paul Russo (University of Miami, USA)

Greta Colombani

A gordian shape of dazzling hue

Serpent Symbolism in Keats's Poetry

V&R unipress

Bibliographic information published by the Deutsche Nationalbibliothek

The Deutsche Nationalbibliothek lists this publication in the Deutsche Nationalbibliografie; detailed bibliographic data are available online: http://dnb.d-nb.de.

ISSN 2365-9173
ISBN 978-3-8471-0775-0

You can find alternative editions of this book and additional material on our website: www.v-r.de

Published with the contribution of the Department of Philology, Literature and Linguistics of the University of Pisa, Dr Simona Beccone's research funds.

BA dissertation, discussed on 24th November 2016, Department of Philology, Literature and Linguistics of the University of Pisa, supervisor Dr Simona Beccone, grade 110/110 cum laude.

© 2017, V&R unipress GmbH, Robert-Bosch-Breite 6, 37079 Göttingen, Germany / www.v-r.de
All rights reserved. No part of this work may be reproduced or utilized in any form or by any means, electronic or mechanical, including photocopying, recording, or any information storage and retrieval system, without prior written permission from the publisher.
Printed in Germany.
Cover image: 'Lamia' Waterhouse, John William; English painter, 1849–1917. 'Lamia', 1909. Oil on canvas, 92.5 x 57.5 cm. Private Collection, courtesy of Christie's. © MONDADORI PORTFOLIO/ AKG Images.
Printed and bound by CPI buchbuecher.de GmbH, Zum Alten Berg 24, 96158 Birkach, Germany.

Printed on aging-resistant paper.

Contents

Acknowledgements 7

Introduction 9

1. Framing the issue 13
   1.1 Occurrences and distribution 13
   1.2 The serpent as 'living symbol' 16

2. Models of creativity 21
   2.1 The Romantic conception of creativity 21
   2.2 Keats's conception of creativity 26
      2.2.1 Imagination 28
      2.2.2 Fancy 37
      2.2.3 Invention 41
      2.2.4 Beauty 42
      2.2.5 Negative Capability 44
      2.2.6 Spontaneous growth *vs* deliberate creation 45

3. Keats's serpents 49
   3.1 Physical characteristics 49
   3.2 Sources 68

4. Textual analyses 81
   4.1 *Endymion* 81
   4.2 Serpents and birds 94
   4.3 *Hyperion* 96
   4.4 *Lamia* 104

Conclusion 119

Bibliography 123
   Primary sources 123
   Secondary sources 124

Acknowledgements

This study is a reworking of my BA dissertation submitted to the Department of Philology, Literature and Linguistics at the University of Pisa. I am very grateful to the University for the opportunities and stimulating environment it has offered me during my years of study.

I would like to thank especially my supervisor, Dr. Simona Beccone (University of Pisa), without whose attentive guidance, priceless advice and willingness this work would not have been possible. She has set an example of excellence as a mentor and scholar. Her enthusiasm and support have always been inspiring.

I would like also to thank Prof. Anthony Leonard Johnson for providing insightful linguistic suggestions, as well as Prof. Paola Partenza (University of Chieti-Pescara) for supporting the publication of my work.

Introduction

Even at first reading, Keats's poetry strikes the reader with the richness of its animal imagery, from the nightingale of the famous ode to the thrush of "O thou whose face hath felt the winter's wind" up to Mrs Reynolds's cat in the less known sonnet. However, no other animal in Keats's whole poetic production shares the serpent's privilege of being at the core of such a long and significant poem as *Lamia*. The fact that a snake is given such prominence comes as no surprise if we agree with Barbara Hannah that "The serpent appears probably more than any other animal in mythology, fairy tales, and primitive religions as well as in the most differentiated faiths" (152). It is, indeed, among the most important as well as most ambiguous symbols that are found across cultures and epochs. If it is true, however, that the centrality of the snake in human imagination has been universally acknowledged and will not be dealt with in the present study, the same does not hold for the important role that the serpent plays in Keats's poems, since its study has been mostly limited to *Lamia* as its most evident instance[1].

As a matter of fact, the representation of animals in literature has lately received a considerable degree of academic attention, and books such as *Kindred Brutes* (2001) by Christine Kenyon-Jones, *Romanticism and Animal Rights* (2003) by David Perkins and *Animality in British Romanticism* (2012) by Peter Heymans have analysed the issue specifically as far as the Romantic period is concerned. All three texts obviously deal with Keats's depictions of animals, but none of them seems to attach particular importance to the serpent[2]. Conversely,

---

1 De Almeida can be considered as an exception, since she is among the few critics to have acknowledged the importance of the serpent also in poems other than *Lamia*. She even devotes to Keats's snakes an entire chapter of her book ("The Ambiguity of Snakes" 182–196), where she interestingly takes into account the influences that classical mythology, medical and naturalist treatises as well as mesmerism may have had on Keats's presentation of serpents.

2 Just as Perkins and Heymans do not even mention the serpent and the former focuses almost

a specific discussion of serpent symbolism in Romantic poetry is found in *Serpent Imagery and Symbolism* (1966) by Lura Nancy and Duilio Pedrini, which has the merit of acknowledging the role of serpent symbolism in the works of the major Romantic poets as well as attempting a classification of it. Even though this taxonomy is undoubtedly useful, as it gathers together almost all the references to snakes in the authors being considered, the extent of its scope tends to smooth over the peculiarities of each writer and, at the same time, to prevent the definition of a somewhat coherent pattern in the serpent imagery of each poet. In other words, the book appears to be a collection rather than an interpretation. As far as Keats is concerned, even the Pedrinis fail to do justice to the actual importance of serpent symbolism in his works as well as to his originality, as they even argue for "the conventionality of many of the serpent images in his poetry" (50).

The present study aims to fill the gap that is produced by the absence of a thorough analysis of serpent symbolism in Keats's poetry. Its relevance, as will be seen, is evident both on a qualitative level – the snake has been said to be the only animal around which a long narrative poem revolves[3] – and on a quantitative one – critics have failed to point out the fact that the serpent is one of the most often mentioned animals in Keats's poetry[4]. In order to correct this neglect, I will not resort to the methodological approach of recent studies, such as those of Kenyon-Jones, Perkins and Heymans, which partly draw on ecocriticism and consider Romantic representations of animals as part of the wider problem of the conception of nature. In these works, it is the way the Romantics saw animals and their relationships with humans to be the main interest, so that both literary and non-literary sources of the period are taken into account as proofs of the views of the time. My approach, instead, will be exclusively literary, as I will not focus on the general Romantic conception of animals, but rather on the specificity of the serpent imagery in Keats's poetry and on its meaning in terms of symbolism.

For this purpose, my chief strategy will be to combine three methodological approaches: a Jungian perspective, a cognitive one, and formal analysis. I will resort to Jung's works for two main reasons. First of all, his definition of 'living symbol' will allow me to specify the terms under which the notion of symbol will

---

exclusively on Keats's birds, which, as will be seen, are the other main component of his animal imagery, so Kenyon-Jones deals with it only as far as *Lamia* is concerned (180–181).

3 As the Pedrinis point out, "Serpent imagery in *Lamia* is organic; there would not be a poem without it" (73).

4 Although the Pedrinis aim to gather together all the images of serpents of the major Romantic poets and have the merit of widening the range of Keatsian references beyond *Lamia*, they still fail to mention all snake occurrences in Keats's poems and limit themselves to *Endymion* III 237–240, 490–502, *Hyperion* I 259–263, *Otho the Great* III ii 152–155, V ii 6–8, several passages from *Lamia* and a rejected stanza of "Ode on Melancholy", where Medusa is mentioned.

be applied to Keats's snakes. This will be discussed in the first chapter, after a statistical survey of all Keats's mentions of serpents, which has never been done before and will point out their quantitative importance. In Keats's poems, the serpent is not presented as a static symbol, as something *standing for* something else that can be identified once and for all. Conversely, it consists in a dynamic symbol which does not possess a fixed referent, but is generated by a constant tension between two opposites, so that their opposition, together with the corresponding significance of the symbol itself, continues to transform while remaining inside the same paradigm, which will be identified as a metapoetic one.

The tension between the two opposites which produces the symbol of the serpent will be shown to parallel precisely the one between the divergent and convergent aspects of the creative process. These two terms are drawn from cognitive studies on creativity, such as *Explaining Creativity* (2006) by Sawyer and *Creativity* (2005) by Pope, which I will refer to in order to derive a descriptive language for the different elements or moments of poetic creation which come into play as far as the snake is concerned. As the metapoetic significance of the serpent obviously depends on Keats's own ideas about the process of poetic composition, the second chapter will be devoted to outlining the main aspects of Keats's conception of creativity, together with the Romantic one, with which Keats has to come to terms in order to develop his own. This overview precedes the actual analysis of the serpent due to its preliminary function: the reader has to be made familiar with Keats's ideas about the creative process as well as the Romantic ones in order to understand their relevance when it comes to the symbol of the snake.

The metapoetic interpretation of serpent symbolism will be accounted for through the second recourse to Jung. The third chapter will focus on physical descriptions of snakes by highlighting their recurring features – a task that has never been carried out systematically before, though this approach has the merit of making it possible to identify some fundamental points for the interpretation of the symbol. At the same time, Keats's characterisation of the serpent will be compared with the archetypal one that is found throughout Jung's production and that has been systematised by Hannah. From their works I will draw some interpretative starting points that will help the task of detecting some correspondences between Keats's representations of the serpent and of imagination. In any case, my perspective will be cultural rather than archetypal: the recurrent attributes that are ascribed to snakes will be considered not as depending on the universal structures of the human mind but as being culturally determined. This means that Keats is confronted with this model of serpent as represented in cultural texts and, in particular, as he was a poet, in literary sources, to whose analysis the second part of the chapter is devoted. Both the comparison with Jung's depiction of the snake and the analysis of the sources show that the elements that Keats innovatively adds, or upon which he lays a greater emphasis, can all be easily traced to a metapoetic significance within Keats's poetic system.

Lastly, after identifying the most frequently recurring characteristics of Keatsian snakes – such as hypnotic eyes, a contorted shape, convulsions and a sense of suffocation – as well as the general frame of reference for their interpretation, in the fourth chapter I will apply these general notions to the most significant occurrences of serpents in Keats's whole poetic production, that is, the episode of Glaucus in Book 3 of *Endymion*, a passage from Book 1 of *Hyperion* and *Lamia*. I will pay particular attention to the formal – for instance, phonosymbolic, metrical and syntactic – aspects of the poems in order to find proofs of my assumptions, and to show how all the levels of the text contribute to conveying the same meaning about snakes. The analysis of the symbol of the serpent in these compositions will then be connected with passages from contemporary letters where Keats expresses his views on the creative process. It will thus be seen how the image of the snake succeeds in expressing some of Keats's most important ideas, as well as his anxieties, about poetic creation – in particular, about the role of imagination and the communication of its insights to the reader – and how the symbol continues to change as it follows the development of his conception of creativity.

1. Framing the issue

1.1 Occurrences and distribution

Animal imagery is quite frequent in Keats's poems as part of the wider, predominant usage of images drawn from the natural world, and the serpent plays an important part in it, even if only the quantitative aspect is taken into account. In the whole corpus of his poetry, the word 'serpent' occurs seventeen times[5] and three more in its plural form[6], while 'snake' is used five times[7]. The main difference between the two terms consists merely in their etymology: while the former comes from Latin through the mediation of the French, the latter has a Germanic derivation and shares the monosyllabic form of many indigenous words. Keats resorts to more specific names too, as he twice mentions the 'adder'[8] and the 'asp'[9], and once 'vipers'[10], even including the mythological 'Python'[11]. Thus, he refers directly to a serpent thirty-one times altogether, which means that it is the animal with the third highest number of occurrences, as it is outnumbered only by 'dove(s)' (42)[12] and the more general 'bird(s)' (32), while it recurs the same number of times as 'eagle' (31). In terms of the number of occurrences, it is immediately followed by 'bee(s)' (25), 'fish(es)' (18), 'lion(s)' (15) and 'nightingale(s)' (14). These data help to map out a pattern which contrasts snakes with birds, as all the animals that exceed in number – or equal – the occurrences of the former belong to the group of the latter. The same op-

---

5 *Endymion* III 240, *Isabella* 412, *Hyperion* I 261, II 45, *Lamia* I 59, 64, 83, 89, 113, 132, 146, 203, II 80 (two times), 298, 305 and *The Fall of Hyperion* I 447.
6 *Endymion* II 875, *Isabella* 190 and "Welcome joy and welcome sorrow" 15.
7 *Endymion* III 494, "Fancy" 57, *Otho the Great* IV i 14 and *Lamia* I 45, 88.
8 "Song of Four Fairies" 68 and *Lamia* II 224.
9 "Welcome joy and welcome sorrow" 17 (in the alternative form of "aspic") and *The Caps and Bells* 197.
10 *Otho the Great* III ii 153.
11 *Endymion* III 530.
12 As was true in the case of all the various kinds of serpents, all different species are included: 'dove(s)' (35), 'hen-dove' (1), 'ring-dove(s)' (5) and 'stock-dove' (1).

position is found in archetypal symbolism too, where the chthonic principle of the snake is considered to be the opposite of the aerial one of the bird[13]. The contrasting relationship between snakes and birds in Keats's poetry, however, will be discussed later.

Furthermore, if it is true that the four most frequently recurring animals in Keats's poems are present in a somewhat similar number of occurrences, these occurrences are distributed in quite different ways. Doves are mentioned in seventeen poems, birds in nineteen and the eagle in fourteen, but snakes appear only in ten different works, and, what is more, almost half of their mentions (15) are, unsurprisingly, concentrated in *Lamia* (1819), which is entirely focused on a serpent. Being at the centre of a whole narration is a privilege the serpent does not share with any other animal apart from the nightingale in the famous ode, which is, however, a far shorter composition. This fact points out how meaningful a symbol the snake is and how powerfully it affected Keats's imagination, as being at the core of an entire poem distances it from being merely decorative imagery.

As far as its chronological distribution is concerned, the serpent is evoked for the first time in Book 1 of *Endymion* (started in April 1817) in the metaphorical neologism "serpentry" (821), whereas it first appears as an actual animal in line 875 of Book 2 (finished by 28 August 1817). Despite being absent from Keats's earlier poetic attempts, it is present until the end of his brief poetic career, as it last occurs in "The Cap and Bells", written between November and December 1819. Snakes, however, are not referred to at regular intervals throughout Keats's poems and two peaks can be identified in Book 3 of *Endymion* (written in September 1817) and, predictably, in *Lamia* (begun on 28 June 1819 and completed by 5 September of the same year). The reasons for these two moments of high concentration, which occur almost two years apart, will be dealt with later, but it is interesting here to note that both works are narrative poems. As a matter of fact, serpents are far more frequent in narrative compositions (25) than in lyrical (4) or dramatic ones (2), which will reveal something about their meta-poetic significance, as different genres respond to distinct laws and require different modes of composition.

Lastly, the considerable presence of serpents in Keats's poems corresponds to their almost total absence in his letters, where the adder is mentioned, but only once. In a letter to Charles Brown dated 22 September 1819, Keats wrote: "If you have anything to gainsay, I shall be even as the deaf adder which stoppeth her ears" (*Letters*, vol. 2, 177). He is here referring to Psalm 58: "Their poison is like the poison of a serpent: they are like the deaf adder that stoppeth her ear; /

---

13 For the rivalry between the serpent and the bird, see Durand 330 and Jung, *Psychology and Alchemy* 292 ("the chthonic principle of the serpent and the aerial principle of the bird").

Which will not hearken to the voice of charmers, charming never so wisely" (4–5). This biblical image of the snake that eludes the charmers by stopping its ears, however, has no echo in the poems, where the focus shifts from the ears to the eyes. In fact, in "Song of Four Fairies" (April 1819) the adder is mentioned in association with its eyes – Dusketha is said to be "Adder-eyed" (68) – and, furthermore, the roles seem to reverse: the adder-like fairy charms (73: "so enchantingly") more than is charmed. More in general, the lack of serpents in the letters suggests that Keats does not need them in the discursive mode found in his prose writings, where he directly verbalises his views on the creative process and discusses them in abstract terms according to the theories of the age. In poetry, instead, he expresses through images what he is experiencing about his own creativity during the poetic act. The difference between the two modes of writing is acknowledged by Keats himself when, in the letter to Bailey about the truth of imagination, he considers "O Sorrow" as "a representation from the fancy of the probable mode of operating in these Matters" (*Letters*, vol. 1, 185), that is, as the poetic expression depending on the imagination of what he has discursively and directly debated in the letter without imaginatively transfiguring it.

The occurrences of serpents in Keats's poems are listed and turned into percentages in the following table in order to make their distribution and their peaks of concentration throughout his poetic production more evident. I have here taken into account not only all the different nouns that are referred to snakes but also neologisms which Keats coins from 'serpent', such as "serpentry" (*Endymion* I 821) and "serpenting" (*Endymion* II 501).

Poem	No. of mentions of serpents	Percentage
Endymion I	1	3 %
Endymion II	1	3 %
Endymion III	4	12.1 %
Isabella	2	6.1 %
"Welcome joy and welcome sorrow"	2	6.1 %
"Fancy"	1	3 %
"Song of Four Fairies"	1	3 %
Hyperion	2	6.1 %
Otho the Great	2	6.1 %
Lamia	15	45.5 %
The Fall of Hyperion	1	3 %
The Caps and Bells	1	3 %

1.2 The serpent as 'living symbol'

If serpent imagery in Keats's poetry is to be interpreted in terms of symbolism, it is necessary to specify that the definition of 'symbol' that I will apply throughout my analysis is the Jungian one, in particular that of 'living symbol', as it makes it possible to account for some of the most important aspects of Keats's representation of serpents. Jung draws a precise distinction between metaphor and symbol. 'Metaphor' derives from the ancient Greek *metapherein*, 'to transport', and it stands for the transfer of the meaning of a word or object to another word or object through analogy. It substitutes a given meaning ('literal') with another one ('figurative') that is clearly determined, so that, given the latter, it is not difficult to recover the former. In other words, metaphors create new meaningful associations by juxtaposing two distant objects, of which one is present and the other absent, and they work thanks to some mimetic relationship[14].

According to the traditional use of the term, 'symbol' – which derives from the ancient Greek *symbállo*, 'to put together' – shares the same substitutive property as 'metaphor', since it refers to an expression that stands for another one. The main difference between the two concepts is that the symbol is arbitrary and, therefore, culturally determined, whereas the metaphor detects a relation of analogy between its two elements. The term is similarly applied to depth psychology, where the symbol is a superficial psychical element that indirectly signifies an in-depth located one. According to Freud, for example, the manifest content of a dream works as a symbol and it has to be interpreted in order to get to the latent one. The true meaning, in fact, is only temporarily hidden because of the censorship of the consciousness, but what is most significant is that the correspondence between the two psychical elements is well-defined and can always be decoded[15].

Jung rejects this notion of symbol, which could be more appropriately referred to as 'sign'[16], and dismisses anything standing for something else that is

---

14 Jung never explicitly defines 'metaphor' as he does, instead, with 'symbol', but its main characteristics emerge throughout his works. For instance, when dealing with the metaphorical processes of dreams, he points out how they work "in accordance with the law of analogy" and how speech itself becomes somewhat indistinct, so that "similar expressions are substituted for one another" (Jung, *Psychogenesis of Mental Disease* 113).

15 In "Symbolism in dreams", Freud defines symbols as "stable translations" (*The Complete Introductory Lectures on Psychoanalysis* 151) and identifies the essence of the symbolic relation with a "comparison" (152) between elements of the dream and elements of the latent dream-thoughts, so that it approaches the notion of "replacement" (*ibidem*). Thus, the symbol in a dream stands for a latent content of the unconscious that can *replace* it thanks to a decoding act.

16 In a note in *Psychological Types* (1921), Jung asserts that "What Freud terms symbols are no more than *signs* for elementary instinctive processes" (63).

univocally determined and fixed as 'dead symbol'. According to him, a symbol is instead 'living' when "it is an expression for something that cannot be characterized in any other or better way" (Jung, *Psychological Types* 474). While a dead symbol possesses only a "historical significance", a symbol lives so long as it is "pregnant with meaning" (475). A living symbol does not work through substitution but through transformation – something is changed into something else. While the traditional symbol and the metaphor refer to something that is already known and substitute it, the living symbol refers to something that is not yet determined and cannot be substituted by it. As a consequence, it can never be entirely decoded.

As far as analytical psychology is concerned, Jung defines the 'living symbol' as a tensional synthesis of the opposites, i.e. "The raw material shaped by thesis and antithesis, and in the shaping of which the opposites are reunited" (480), so that "The energy created by the tension of opposites [...] flows into the mediatory product" (479). This definition derives from Jung's idea that psychic life is a self-regulating system that draws its energy from the unresolved tension between opposite elements, such as conscious and unconscious, masculine and feminine, rationality and pulsionality. In the symbol, the opposites come together (*coniunctio oppositorum*) but they never achieve a static synthesis where they cancel each other out. Both exist in a relationship that is polar rather than mutually exclusive. They define each other by maintaining a dynamic tension and their symbolic representation continues to be subject to transformation, as what it stands for can never be completely grasped. In accordance with these definitions, Jung ascribes four characteristics to living symbols, which are all related one to another and which will be here applied to the serpent in Keats's poetry in order to prove that it is precisely a 'living symbol'[17].

The first is 'indicativity', which means that the symbol does not merely 'mean' something but rather 'actuates meanings'. It hints at something that cannot be translated in rationally defined terms as it always eludes them. If the symbol had a semantically circumscribed meaning, it would no longer be able to arouse new meanings, which is its pragmatic function. Thus, the symbol endlessly refers to something that is not yet known and that is always beyond. In Keats's poems, the serpent does not have a precise, fixed meaning, in the way dead symbols or metaphors do. In fact, the serpent is not a metaphor since it does not stand for something else that is univocally determined through a mimetic relationship[18]. For instance, 'serpent' does not mean 'treacherous person', alluding to poi-

---

17 As a matter of fact, Jung himself points out that the serpent is usually a symbol, "not an allegory or a metaphor, for its own peculiar form is symbolic in itself" (Jung, *Aion* 188).
18 Actually, it will be seen how Keats also uses serpents as metaphors in a more conventional way, as in *Otho the Great* and *The Cap and Bells*.

sonous snakes concealed in the grass, as happens in Virgil's "latet anguis in herba" (*Eclogues* III 93). 'Serpent' has no clear semantic equivalent, but it appears every time as a powerful image that is able to express new meanings, as is proven by the fact that it remains productive during the main part of Keats's poetic career, from *Endymion* to *The Fall of Hyperion*.

The second is 'the decomposability of the whole and the composability of the polar elements in a non-synthetic unity'. While the consciousness discerns and separates the opposites and relies on dead symbols, a part of the unconscious – the so-called 'creative psyche' – constantly attempts to put them together in a relation of creative tension that preserves the two distinct elements and never unifies them in a synthetic third one. That the symbol of the serpent in Keats includes opposite elements within itself is clearly shown by its bivalent nature. Regarding its axiological status, in fact, the serpent is never entirely positive nor entirely negative. It is both a smothering, deceiving, predatory creature and, at the same time, a benevolent being endowed with a superior knowledge. The critics still argue about which of the two Lamia most authentically is[19], but even when one aspect seems dominant, the other is never absent. In the third book of *Endymion*, for instance, a fire similar to the eye of a snake helps Glaucus to discover the truth about Circe, but this fire is also somehow related to the seductive sorceress. In addition, the psychic state of the narrator or the character who deals with the serpent is marked by ambivalence, as he is simultaneously fascinated and repelled by the animal. These two connotations of the serpent always coexist, even if in varying proportions, and the tension between the two is never resolved.

The third can be referred to as 'decisionality', which means that a symbol is neither a symbol in itself nor can it be interpreted as one according to one's own will. Instead, "whether a thing is a symbol or not depends chiefly on the attitude of the observing consciousness; for instance, on whether it regards a given fact not merely as such but also as an expression for something unknown" (Jung, *Psychological Types* 475). The serpent does not intrinsically nor necessarily always mean what it means to Keats, but, at the same time, what it stands for is not something Keats individually decides. It is in culture that he finds an image corresponding to what is still unknown to his consciousness and yet he wishes to express about the mystery of his own creativity. The power of this cultural image is still alive to him and acts on his mind so that it is perceived as a symbol. For instance, all the characteristics of the serpent that have been mentioned in the

---

19 Perkins and Patterson's axiologically opposite judgements on Lamia can be quoted as an example of this critical controversy. While the former asserts that "Lamia is, after all, a serpent, and however loving she may be, she still preys on him" (Perkins in Hill 193), the latter defines her as a "feminine creature of warmth and appeal, genuinely involved in her love for Lycius" (Patterson 192).

previous paragraph are found by Keats in literary tradition, from the evil snake in the Bible and in *Paradise Lost* to Cadmus and Harmonia's metamorphosis in two benevolent serpents in Sandys's Ovid.

The fourth characteristic is 'transcendence', that is, the continuous exceeding of assigned meanings. The 'transcendent function' unifies conscious and unconscious by overstepping their boundary, which, however, is never cancelled but only shifted. This function works also within the symbol, since the latter allows some unconscious contents to become conscious but cannot exist outside its antithetical paradigm. As a consequence, the two opposites continue to undergo transformation, but their paradigm is always confirmed. This last point is closely related to the first. As the presence of the serpent in Keats's poems always takes on new meanings that are partly unknown to the author himself, such meanings cannot but spring from the unconscious. This is also proved by the fact that there are almost no recurrences of serpents in the letters, where the demands of writing are different due to the different genre. When he is writing letters, Keats tends to verbalise directly what he wishes to say about his view of the creative process, whereas in poetry, in line with the Romantic conception of creativity, he is more closely linked with his unconscious, so that what he does instead is use symbols to give expression to what he is experiencing at the moment and cannot be entirely grasped. The tension between unconscious and conscious contents, however, is never resolved. The elements found to be in mutual opposition through the symbol of the serpent continue to change, but they all belong to the same paradigm, which is a metapoetic one. The metapoetic nature of the frame of reference of serpent symbolism will be made clear through the analysis of snakes' characteristics that Keats stresses in their depiction, but, since the metapoetic interpretation is obviously based on his own view of the creative process, the next chapter will be devoted to Keats's conception of creativity and to the Romantic one, in relation to which he developed his own.

2. Models of creativity

2.1 The Romantic conception of creativity

The Romantic model of creativity was developed at the end of the 18th century and was dominant throughout the 19th century. As a matter of fact, it is still rather popular today, as some of the most widespread myths about creativity originated in the Romantic Movement and survive in spite of new scientific explanations that point in other directions[20]. The Romantic idea of creativity is, indeed, a double-edged concept, as it applies both to a historically specific theory of artistic creation and to a more general pattern of beliefs which recur over the centuries in opposition to the rationalist conception. Just as Rationalism is the belief that creativity is generated by the conscious, deliberating, rational mind, Romanticism is the belief that creativity springs from unconscious, irrational forces within the artist. The Romantic revolution in the late 18th century proceeded from this same opposition and rejected the previous rationalist view of art, which had its roots in Aristotle's theory and had been further developed during the Enlightenment. The Romantic conception of creativity – and from now on the phrase will be used in its historical sense – revolved around the idea of the artist as a privileged and isolated individual who, inspired by some mysterious force beyond his control, expresses and communicates his[21] unique vision through his own art. The implications of this assertion will be now analysed in detail.

First of all, as opposed to the rationalists of the Augustan age, the Romantics valued imagination above reason. According to what P.B. Shelley propounds in his *A Defence of Poetry* (1821), which can be considered as his manifesto of Romantic poetics, poetry itself is but "the expression of the Imagination" (511). In this essay, Shelley draws a neat distinction between reason and imagination:

---

20 See Sawyer, especially chapter 2, for an insightful analysis of the origin of today's creativity myths and the evolution of the conceptions of creativity over time.
21 I will use male pronouns, as Romantic mythologies are primarily limited to male artists.

the former is the principle of analysis and deals with the relations of one thought to another as distinct and known objects, whereas the latter is the principle of synthesis, colours those thoughts with its own light and combines them to create new ones. While reason focuses on the differences between things, imagination aims to detect their similarities. Shelley goes on to affirm that poetry as the expression of the imagination differs from reasoning also because it cannot be exerted according to one's own will. The mind in creation is subject to "some invisible influence", a power that "arises from within" (531) and can neither be controlled nor predicted by the poet's conscious mind. This is the Romantic view of the artist writing under the command of spontaneous inspiration as opposed to the Augustan theory of poetic composition "by labour and study" (*ibidem*).

Although Shelley further developed these ideas in a personal way, they constituted a background for all the Romantics. For instance, ten years later Mary Shelley described her first inspiration for *Frankenstein* in similar terms: "I did not sleep, nor could I be said to think. My imagination, unbidden, possessed and guided me, gifting the successive images that arose in my mind with a vividness far beyond the usual bounds of reverie" (Mary Shelley 9). Imagination arises when the artist's mind is in a heightened state of consciousness, and, at the same time, it helps to bring about this state while producing an "acute mental vision" (*ibidem*). This idea is not completely new. It has its roots in the Platonic *enthousiasmos*, that is, the condition of 'divine madness' associated with poetic practice in ancient Greece. The main difference is that the artist is now stirred to this condition of almost ecstatic inspiration not by a god or an external muse but by his own unconscious. It is noteworthy in this regard that the first recorded use of the phrase 'the unconscious' in English is by S.T. Coleridge in his "On Poesy or Art" (*Biographia Literaria*, vol. 2, 258).

To sum up, the Romantics generally ascribed creativity to imagination – with its unifying function and its unexpected analogical associations – rather than to the logical and rational way of thinking of the conscious mind. In modern terms, the wandering, free-flowing, non-linear mental processes of divergent thinking were preferred to the focusing, systematic, linear approach of convergent thinking[22]. As a result, the work of art was less the result of the artist's deliberating will than an outburst of inspiration from within, similar to a message dictated by someone else.

Furthermore, Romanticism rejected the traditional mimetic theory of art. If it

---

22 In reality, psycho-cognitive studies reveal that both mental processings are active during creativity. As Sawyer points out, "Creative achievement requires a complex combination of both divergent and convergent thinking, and creative people are good at switching back and forth at different points in the creative process" (45).

is true that the source of creation is the inner vision produced in the artist's mind by imagination, it is clear that art does not depict external objects, nor does it imitate nature. Imagination is a creative faculty rather than a mimetic one and this shift from external sources of creativity to internal ones is among the most important innovations of Romantic poetics. Nevertheless, having a vision, unique though it may be, is not enough to allow an author to write a poem. This vision needs to be expressed and communicated to the reader by means of language.

In order to understand how this passage works according to the Romantic poetics, I will refer to the most famous theoretical text of the movement, that is, the preface to the 1802 edition of the *Lyrical Ballads* by William Wordsworth. Here poetry is defined as "the spontaneous overflow of powerful feelings" which "takes its origin from emotion recollected in tranquillity" (266). Again, the act of creation is described as an unpremeditated regression to a state of consciousness dominated by emotion and instinct, even though Wordsworth acknowledges a subordinate role to thought as well. In particular, he stresses the importance of one of its components, which consists in the memory of past events stored in the subject's mind[23]. As the poet is "a man speaking to men" (255), however, he still wishes to communicate this overflow of feelings to the readers and to share those same emotions with them. This ability is known as the Romantic notion of sympathy. Thanks to sympathy, the poet is able to "bring his feelings near to those of the persons whose feelings he describes" (256) and to empathise with them, so that these emotions can be transmitted to the reader in an unmediated, instinctive way[24]. As a result, the outer communication of the artist's feelings is as spontaneous as their inner overflow.

This kind of poetic expression implies a revolution in the language, too[25]. Wordsworth – as well as the other Romantics – rejected 'poetic diction', that is, the highly codified style of writing used in Classical and Augustan poetry. Being rich in uncommon erudite words and rhetorical devices as well as requiring a skilful craftsmanship, poetic diction was perceived by the Romantics as artificial and divorced from nature. In its place, the choice fell on "a selection of the language of men in a state of vivid sensation" (*Lyrical Ballads* 254). This se-

---

23 "Poems to which any value can be attached were never produced on any variety of subjects but by a man, who being possessed of more than usual organic sensibility, had also thought long and deeply. For our continued influxes of feeling are modified and directed by our thoughts, which are indeed the representatives of all our past feelings" (246).
24 Zimmerman associates this same quotation from Wordsworth with the notion of sympathy (29) and explores its role in the communication of the poet's personal feelings to a reader (30–34).
25 See Doležel, chapter 4, for an in-depth analysis of the idea of poetic language in Wordsworth and Coleridge.

lection needs to be made "with true taste and feeling" (*ibidem*) in order to avoid anything vulgar and mean in poetic composition. According to Wordsworth, only ordinary language with a certain colouring of imagination allows for the authentic expression of a mind agitated by natural affections and powerful feelings. This was the way of writing of the earliest poets before the new abstract language of poetic diction was codified, based on the mechanical adoption of figures of speech that had no connection whatsoever with nature. Romantic poets wished to return to that original condition, as the closer a man is to nature, the stronger his power of imagination grows. The consequent idea that primitives and their equivalent in modern society – children – are more creative than average people is another Romantic myth[26]. In the first section of his *Prelude* (1799), for instance, Wordsworth identifies the child's capability of feeling in harmony with nature with "the first / Poetic spirit of our human life" that is "By uniform control of after years, / In most, abated or suppressed; in some [obviously the poets], / Through every change of growth and of decay, / Pre-eminent till death" (260–265).

More in general, Romantics preferred a highly personal style to the conventions of poetic diction in order to communicate their insights in the most authentic possible way, where 'authentic' stands for 'genuine, unfeigned, presenting the characteristics of the original' (*OED*) and, consequently, 'truthfully reproducing the poet's original experience'. Those conventions derive from the works of previous poets, and poetic diction also stands for tradition. The Augustans believed that poetic composition had to follow rules which had been codified in the past and thus modelled much of their works on the Classics. By contrast, the Romantics valued individual talent and originality above the mastery of tradition. If it is true that Romantic art does not imitate nature, it does not imitate previous art either. This change in ideas is reflected by a corresponding change in the meaning of the word 'original' itself. Until half way through the 18th century it had meant 'from the beginning, former, ancient' (*OED*), but from then on the dominant meaning has shifted to 'fresh, new, novel, unexpected' (*OED*)[27]. Edward Young's *Conjectures on Original Composition* (1759) marks the turning point and draws a Romantic distinction between 'Imitations' and 'Originals' in favour of the latter. The two are contrasted through an organic metaphor that is rather common among the Romantics and will be

---

26 According to Horne, the early Romantic poets expanded Rousseau's construction of the child of nature, so that "the Romantic child came to represent the inherent creative powers that the adult poet must reclaim in order to create art, powers that emerge in an all-sufficing solitude" (95).
27 See Pope 57–60.

found in Keats too[28]. "An original may be said to be of a vegetal nature; it rises spontaneously from the vital root of genius; it grows, it is not made: imitations are often a sort of manufacture wrought up by those mechanics, art, and labour, out of preexistent materials not their own" (349). Artists who imitate previous artists always deserve less recognition, as they have to share their glory with those whom they imitate. Originals, instead, are worthy of more praise, because, being entirely novel, they make a greater contribution to the advancement of literature. The Romantic focus is entirely on the individuality of the artist and the novelty of his creations compared to previous works of art.

Therefore, the Romantic artist is portrayed as an exceptional individual who creates in isolation and responds only to inspiration. He is endowed with a finer sensibility than that of the average individual, which allows him to feel more deeply and to be more sensitive to the suggestions of imagination. He also matches the melancholic type, which is distinguished by introversion, pensiveness, sensitivity, restlessness, love for solitude, moodiness, elegiac sadness, gloominess. Before the advent of Romanticism, in fact, the notion of melancholy had already moved from an illness caused by excess of black bile to an essentially subjective mood or disposition[29]. Moreover, the Romantic artist is often believed to be misunderstood by his contemporaries, with his talent often remaining unacknowledged during his lifespan. At this point, the myth of the genius is born. So too, 'genius' is a term that underwent a crucial shift in meaning during the second half of the century. It moved away from its spiritual and collective senses associated with a kin or a place (e.g. *genius loci*) towards the modern sense of 'an exceptionally creative or clever individual' (*OED*)[30]. According to Coleridge in his *Biographia Literaria* (1817), 'genius' differs from 'talent', as the former is a "creative, and self-sufficing power", whereas the latter consists of "the faculty of appropriating and applying the knowledge of others" (vol. 1, 20), that is, of using tradition and conventional means to fulfil its purpose. Although this exact distinction between the two terms was not shared by all the Romantics, it is helpful in gaining a better insight into their conception of genius, as it points out its innate nature, whereas talent can be acquired through study and practice, and the fact that it draws its means from within, unlike talent that finds them outside.

As far as genre is concerned, Romantics favoured poetry – above all lyric poetry –, even though both Wordsworth and Shelley insisted that they used 'Poetry' in its wider sense to include all literary artistic expressions without any

---

28 For the use of metaphors of natural growth to represent natural genius and spontaneous, unconscious creation, see Abrams, chapter 8.
29 See Radden 29–32.
30 See Pope 101–107.

distinction whatsoever between prose and metre. This is the reason why 'poetic' has sometimes been used as a synonym for 'artistic' or 'literary' even in what has been written above. Nevertheless, it is not by chance that the major Romantic writers were all poets in the strictest sense of the term. Lyric poetry is a more fitting genre than narrative poetry or prose to give expression to the poet's own personal feelings and to his imaginative insights, and it seemingly requires less rational effort than constructing a coherent plot. Ultimately, a rather brief lyric poem is more likely to convey the impression of a spontaneous overflow of inspiration that has been put equally spontaneously into words.

These are the key points of the Romantic conception of creativity, but it would be misleading to believe that Romantic writers actually composed by exactly following these dictates. For instance, a closer study of Romantic poetry reveals a more consistent amount of conscious craftsmanship than might be expected, even in poems whose composition was claimed to have occurred under the effect of drugs, such as Coleridge's *Kubla Khan*[31]. What has been described so far is thus less a truthful description of the creative process than its Romantic theoretical modelling. It is, however, meaningful for the present study, as it is exactly the set of ideas about creativity which Keats was confronted with in his aim to become a poet.

2.2 Keats's conception of creativity

Keats mainly developed his view of creativity during the early years of his poetic career after quitting medicine and devoting himself completely to poetry. Unlike other Romantic writers, such as Wordsworth (Preface to the 1802 edition of the *Lyrical Ballads*), Coleridge (*Biographia Literaria*, 1817) and Shelley (*A Defence of Poetry*, 1840), he left no theoretical text on the subject, so that his thoughts have to be inferred from his letters and poems, especially those written between 1817 and 1818. Aspiring to be a poet in the early 19th century, Keats could not but look to the Romantic model and its notions of imagination and feeling. With the Romantics – in particular, Leigh Hunt, whom he chose as his first guide in the literary world – the young Keats shared a deep aversion to the neoclassical rigidity of Augustan style. In "Sleep and Poetry" (1816) he accused the Augustans of being "a thousand handicraftsmen" (200) disguised as poets, "nurtured

---

[31] See Coleridge's preface to the poem: "The Author continued for about three hours in a profound sleep, at least of the external sense, during which time he has the most vivid confidence, that he could not have composed less than from two to three hundred lines; if that indeed can be called composition in which all the images rose up before him as *things*, with a parallel production of the correspondent expressions, without any sensation or consciousness of effort" (*Poetical Works* 296).

by foppery and barbarism" (182) and unable to feel true Beauty, as the latter can be achieved only through the powers of imagination. In fact, he also agreed with the Romantics' belief in the predominance of emotion and imagination over cold reason and speculative thinking – in Keats's terms "consequitive reasoning" (*Letters*, vol. 1, 185) – as means of knowledge as well as sources of poetry.

In a letter to Reynolds dated 19 February 1818, Keats expressed his acceptance of Romantic principles through the famous metaphor of the spider: "it appears to me that almost any Man may like the Spider spin from his own inwards his own airy Citadel" (*Letters*, vol. 1, 231). Keats shows here that he shared the Romantic idea that the materials of creation are to be found within the artist. The poet has to rely only on his inner faculties, as excellence in art is not achieved through study or imitation, that is, by looking at outer sources of inspiration, but by giving expression to his own individual vision. Keats draws the metaphor of the spider from Swift's *The Battle of Books* (1704), where the spider who builds its citadel with "Materials extracted altogether out of my own Person" (231) stands for the Moderns, whereas the bee who gains what it has "by infinite Labor, and search, and ranging thro' every Corner of Nature" (234) represents the Ancients. However, if Swift favours the bee that gathers its material from nature in line with an 18th-centrury point of view, Keats overturns Swift's judgement and praises the spider above the bee[32], the moderns above the ancients.

Before analysing in detail the key concepts of Keats's model of creativity and their debt to Romanticism, I had better start by saying that the relationship between Keats and his Romantic models is not free from ambiguity. Keats struggled to be acknowledged as a poet by his contemporaries[33] and, in order to do so, he conformed to what a poet was meant to be according to the Romantics, who were the literary authorities of the time. Nevertheless, Keats always sit on the sidelines of the literary establishment, partly due to his social background and education, and partly to his poetic choices. In a sense, he followed the Romantic principles too literally and ended up being more Romantic than the Romantics. Keats aimed to pursue his own artistic independence even when it led far from the Romantic path, but he soon found out that the Romantics valued in-

---

32 See below the passage of Keats's letter to Reynolds dated 19 February 1818, where the condition of the bee is rejected, this time in favour of that of the flower (*Letters*, vol. 1, 232).
33 His aspiration is particularly clear when he speaks of fame, a term which implies a public acknowledgement. "If I think of fame of poetry it seems a crime to me, and yet I must do so or suffer," he writes in a letter to Dilke (*Letters*, vol. 1, 369), when even the closeness to his brother's suffering cannot divert him from his purpose. His desire is also revealed by his doubts: "These last two day however I have felt more confident – I have asked myself so often why I should be a Poet more than other Men, – seeing how great a thing it is, – how great things are to be gained by it – What a thing to be in the Mouth of Fame" (*Letters*, vol. 1, 139). Moreover, he writes to his editor regarding his poetic choices: "I was never afraid of failure; for I would sooner fail than not be among the greatest" (*Letters*, vol. 1, 374).

dividuality and personal expression more in theory than in practice. If it is true that they rejected poetic diction and the strict rules of neoclassical poetry, they actually substituted them with a new diction and new rules, which may be less explicit and rigid but not less effective. This new diction derived precisely from the conception of creativity that has been considered in the previous chapter.

Keats had been confronted with this paradox of Romanticism and especially with the related issue of genre since writing *Endymion*, his first considerable poetic experiment. On 8 October 1817 he quoted to Bailey a letter he had previously written to his brother George, where he deals with Hunt's criticism regarding long poems. Hunt, who shared with the Romantics a preference for rather brief lyric poems, wondered why Keats should endeavour to write a long one and, what is more, to choose the genre of mythological romance, which does not conform to the Romantic conventions. Keats proudly asserts his right to artistic independence: "You see Bailey how independant my writing has been – Hunts dissuasion was of no avail – I refused to visit Shelley, that I might have my own unfettered scope" (*Letters*, vol. 1, 170). Although Keats was strongly influenced by Hunt's poetry at the beginning of his career, he did not feel comfortable with "the Reputation of Hunt's elevé" (*ibidem*) and struggled to free himself from any conditioning, including that of a young fellow poet such as P.B. Shelley.

Furthermore, Keats goes on to justify his choices by making poetic assumptions: "a long Poem is a test of Invention which I take to be the Polar Star of Poetry, as Fancy is the sails, and Imagination the Rudder. Did our great Poets ever write short Pieces? I mean in the shape of Tales – This same invention seems i<n>deed of late Years to have been forgotten as a Poetical excellence" (*ibidem*). Imagination cooperates here with two other poetic faculties, and this is the only case where the three terms occur together. While imagination directs the poet's mind during its divergent wandering and fancy provides the actual means for its progression, invention seems, oddly, to be elevated above the other two poetic powers as the actual guide of the creative process. I will now focus on the different but sometimes interrelated uses of the three terms in Keats's works and on their development during his poetic career by first considering his probable sources in the writings of Wordsworth and Coleridge.

2.2.1 Imagination

In the Preface to his collected *Poems* of 1815, Wordsworth defines the powers that are required for the production of poetry, namely observation, description, sensibility, reflection, imagination, fancy, invention and judgement, some of which recur in Keats's letters too. Wordsworth mainly focuses on the properties of imagination and fancy, and draws a distinction between the two. Both faculties aim "to aggregate and to associate, to evoke and to combine" (*Poetical Works* 755), but the laws according to which they work are different. Wordsworth rejects the 18th-century idea of imagination as dealing with mental faithful images of absent external objects, and considers it rather as denoting "processes of creation and compositions" (753). When these processes act on an individual image, they consist in "conferring additional properties upon an object, or abstracting from it some of those which it actually possesses, and thus enabling it to react upon the mind which hath performed the process, like a new existence" (754). Not only is imagination a transformative power[34] – it is a creative one, too. It modifies the materials which it makes use of in order to create something new. Fancy, instead, does not alter its objects, but the main differences among the two faculties are more evident when they deal with more than one image in conjunction. The comparisons framed by imagination gradually and increasingly strike the mind with "a sense of the truth of the likeness", as the resemblance depends "less upon outline of form and feature [...] than upon inherent and internal [...] properties" (755). Conversely, fancy scatters images with "rapidity and profusion" and links them through curious but superficial subtlety as well as fortuitous combinations in order to surprise and amuse the reader. Its law is "as capricious as the accidents of things" (*ibidem*). As a result, the influence of fancy is as transitory and unstable as the influence of imagination is lasting and constant.

The most famous distinction between imagination and fancy, however, is that drawn by Coleridge in his *Biographia Literaria* (1817). Coleridge asserts that his conclusions differ from those of Wordsworth; for instance, he denies any combinatory or associative power to imagination and ascribes it solely to fancy. First of all, Coleridge distinguishes between two types of imagination. He calls 'primary imagination' "the living Power and prime Agent of all human Perception" (*Biographia Literaria*, vol. 1, 202), that is, the human faculty of perceiving the outer world through the senses. By contrast, the 'secondary imagination' is a higher power whose aim is "to idealize and to unify" (*ibidem*). It does not perceive the world but rather "recreate[s]" (*ibidem*) it by forging the images and sensations supplied by the primary imagination into a new unity. While the primary imagination is a spontaneous act of the human mind in facing the world and thus unconscious and involuntary, the secondary imagination coexists with "the conscious will" (*ibidem*) and is exerted only by the artist. Furthermore, it is the latter that Coleridge contrasts with fancy, which is considered by him to be a

---

34 Wordsworth had already stressed the transformative power of imagination in his Preface to the *Lyrical Ballads*, where he refers to "a certain colouring of imagination, whereby ordinary things should be presented to the mind in an unusual aspect" (244).

lesser, somewhat mechanical faculty. Fancy is defined as "a mode of memory" that receives "all its materials ready made from the law of association". It works through a combinatory principle and it differs from imagination because it brings "together images dissimilar in the main by some point or more of likeness" (Coleridge, *Lectures 1808–1819*, vol. 1, 67), but these images continue to retain their individual properties and never achieve the unity provided by the secondary imagination.

Keats first refers to imagination in the already mentioned "Sleep and Poetry", which dates back to the late 1816 and where imagination is identified with the main element of the renewed poetic blooming following the period of decline in the 18th century in accordance with the Romantic view of the history of poetry. If the Augustan poets held to "a poor, decrepit standard" (204) and never let imagination "freely fly / As she was wont of old", the present situation seems to lead to a positive reversal: "the imagination / Into most lovely labyrinths will be gone, / And they shall be accounted poet-kings / Who simply tell the most heart-easing things" (265–268). In both cases, the activities of imagination are rendered through verbs of movement, but, while in the former imagination flies unconstrained through the air, in the latter its movement follows a labyrinthine path that stands for the non-linear process of poetic composition, as also in "On Receiving a Laurel Crown from Leigh Hunt" (1817; "delphic labyrinth", 3). The labyrinth as poetic image is an important point to which I will return later, but here I will focus on the image of a free wandering imagination. 'Wandering', in fact, is precisely the metaphor used by Romantic poets to represent the so-called divergent thinking as in the famous incipit of Wordsworth's "I wandered lonely as a cloud", which Keats echoes in his "Ode to Psyche" ("I wandered in a forest thoughtlessly", 7). Here, Keats explicitly compares the mental state preceding the poetic vision with the absence of 'Thought', a term that usually means discursive thinking to him. In other words, imagination arises within the poet when his mind is not bound by the constraints of rationality, and is free to wander without any predetermined destination, which is how imagination itself proceeds.

Keats returned to the subject a year later in one of his best-known letters to Benjamin Bailey dated 22 November 1817, which is also his most in-depth analysis of the nature of imagination. He introduces the topic in the following way:

> O I wish I was certain of the end of all your troubles as that of your momentary start about the authenticity of the Imagination. I am certain of nothing but of the holiness of the Heart's affections and the truth of Imagination – What the imagination seizes as Beauty must be truth – whether it existed before or not – for I have the same Idea of all our Passions as of Love they are all in their sublime, creative of essential Beauty (*Letters*, vol. 1, 184).

This paragraph can be considered as the core of Keats's whole argument, as it establishes the intrinsic connections between imagination, beauty and truth, even though the key role is played by the former[35]. Keats assumes that imagination is always directed to beauty, or rather, using his own words, imagination "seizes" beauty, a verb whose meaning ranges from a physical grabbing to an all mental understanding. Here this seizing can take two forms, which are expressed in the most important clause "whether it existed before or not". Either imagination perceives the beauty of things that actually are or it envisages the beauty of those which are yet to come. In other words, as the philosopher John Sallis brilliantly points out[36], imagination is a twofold faculty that is at the same time perceptive and creative. Its creative potential is highlighted again in the following sentence where beauty is explicitly said to be created, but this time by passions. Keats had already linked imagination with "Heart's affections" in order to convey the idea that the imaginative faculty works together with the emotional one, and more precisely that the latter provides some of the materials upon which the former acts. Wordsworth too considers emotions as objects of imagination[37], but Keats never refers to this faculty as a combinatory one and is more influenced by the ideas in Coleridge's *Biographia Literaria*, which was published in the same year as this letter. Keats finds in Coleridge an acknowledgement of the twofold nature of imagination – perceptive and creative – but he does not agree with ascribing these two ways of functioning to two distinct faculties. Furthermore, Keats rejects the idea of a conscious, voluntary imagination, such as Coleridge's secondary imagination, and he depicts it rather as an unconscious, involuntary activity that functions under an intensity of feelings. Instead of being deliberately exerted through the will, it arises spontaneously in the mind of the poet as a dream; thus Keats goes on to say:

> The Imagination may be compared to Adam's dream – he awoke and found it truth. I am the more zealous in this affair, because I have never yet been able to perceive how any thing can be known for truth by consequitive reasoning – and yet it must be – Can it be that even the greatest Philosopher ever <when> arrived at his goal without putting aside numerous objections – However it may be, O for a Life of Sensations rather than Thoughts! (185).

Keats refers here to Book 8 of *Paradise Lost*, where God makes Adam sleep, so that he closes his eyes but leaves open "the Cell / Of Fancy [here 'fancy' is the

---

35 Douka-Kabitoglou sees imagination in this passage not only as "the central issue" but also as "a middle term" (126) that makes it possible to establish a relationship between beauty and truth. However, she interprets this relation and, in general, Keats's poetics in Platonic terms.
36 See Sallis 16–20.
37 "I have given in these unfavourable times evidence of exertions of this faculty upon its worthiest objects, the external universe, the moral and religious sentiments of Man, his natural affections, and his acquired passions" (Wordsworth, *Poetical Works* 755).

same as 'imagination'] my internal sight, by which / Abstract as in a trance" (460–462) he sees Eve only to wake up and "behold her, not far off, / Such as I saw her in my dream" (481–482). This comparison between imagination and Adam's dream is significant mainly for two reasons. First, it points out how imagination occurs in a state of hightened consciousness and in terms of intuitive vision while dismissing discursive, rational thinking as an inadequate means to acquire truth in the following sentence. Secondly, it identifies the truth of imagination with an outer realisation of the inner vision. Creation and perception intertwine again, since the creations of imagination need to be perceived outside the mind in order to be acknowledged as true. Keats concludes by expanding this point:

> have you never by being surprised with an old Melody – in a delicious place – by a delicious voice, fe[l]t over again your very speculations and surmises at the time it first operated on your soul – do you not remember forming to yourself the singer's face more beautiful that [*for* than] it was possible and yet with the elevation of the Moment you did not think so – even then you were mounted on the Wings of Imagination so high – that the Prototype must be here after – that delicious face you will see (185).

As Adam awakes and sees the Eve of his dream in front of him, so the listener is destined to behold the imagined face of the singer and recognise it as a repetition and actualisation of his imaginings. Keats returned to the same terms and themes expressed in this letter in the one to Taylor dated 30 January 1818, where he wrote about the "Pleasure Thermometer" in *Endymion*: "The whole thing must I think have appeared to you, who are a consequitive Man, as a thing almost of mere words – but I assure you that when I wrote it, it was a regular stepping of the Imagination towards a Truth" (*Letters*, vol. 1, 218).

However, in the following months, his blind faith in imagination seems somehow to have dimmed as Keats went through a period of transition where he started questioning his Romantic beliefs. Imagination is depicted for the first time as an ambiguous rather than completely positive power in the verse letter he sent to his friend and fellow-poet Reynolds on 25 March 1818.

> Oh, never will the prize,
> High reason and the lore of good and ill,
> Be my award. Things cannot to the will
> Be settled, but they tease us out of thought.
> Or is it that imagination brought
> Beyond its proper bound, yet still confined,
> Lost in a sort of Purgatory blind,
> Cannot refer to any standard law
> Of either earth or heaven? It is a flaw
> In happiness to see beyond our bourn –
> It force us in summer skies to mourn;
> It spoils the singing of the nightingale. (74–85)

Keats starts by pointing out the limitations of rational thinking, as he is used to, but this time he does not celebrate imagination in its place. What he does do is wonder whether the imagination does not turn out to be a dangerous resource when it is brought beyond its "proper bound", that is, when it is free to wander and not subjected to any law. This possibility of unconstrained movement and action, which was something to be wished for in "Sleep and Poetry", is now seen as a threat to human happiness, which is identified here with the enjoyment of the present moment without trying to overstep the limits of our immediate perception and understanding. If imagination is not somehow controlled, it can indulge in morose pictures even in the loveliest scenery, thanks to its ability to make present what is not[38]. This ability is what determines the liminal nature of imagination as described in these lines. Imagination, in fact, belongs to heaven, i.e. another world, since it is able to create things that did not exist before – as seen in the letter to Bailey –, but, as it is a human faculty, it creates them in our world, so it is confined to earth.

Imagination is again referred to as something interfering with happiness in the letter about women that Keats wrote to Bailey a few months later, on 10 June 1818: "Women must want Imagination and they may thank God for it – and so m[a]y we that a delicate being can feel happy without any sense of crime" (*Letters*, vol. 1, 293). The idea of a negative imagination, instead, returned in "On Visiting the Tomb of Burns", written on 1 July 1818 during his tour of Scotland, and seemingly almost a continuation of the verse letter to Reynolds. In the sonnet, the poetic persona beholds the summer, although just begun, as if already haunted by the gloom of winter, and knowing that it has only a short life. He is not able to rejoice in or with the surrounding nature, whose beauty he acknowledges, but only as a beauty that remains cold to him.

> All is cold beauty; pain is never done:
> For who has mind to relish, Minos-wise,[39]
> The real of beauty, free from that dead hue
> Sickly imagination and sick pride
> Cast wan upon it! […] (8–12)

If imagination gets sick, not only is it no longer able to seize beauty, but it actually becomes an obstacle to achieving real beauty. The deadly hue that envelops everything is, in fact, not a property of the landscape but a quality

---

38 The idea of imagination as vision of something that is not physically present is the most ordinary, non-poetic meaning which is ascribed to the term throughout Keats's poems and letters: see *Endymion* III 1008–1009; *Letters*, vol. 1, 341; vol. 2, 78, 218, 351, and 360.

39 For these two lines I maintain the punctuation of the original draft in the letter to Tom dated 1 July 1818, as transcribed by Jeffrey, unlike Allott, who interprets "For who […] upon it!" as a relative.

conferred by imagination. In those days, Keats was meditating about imagination and its role in the poetic fate of Burns. On 7 July he wrote to his brother Tom: "how sad it is when a luxurious imagination is obliged in self defence to deaden its delicacy in vulgarity, and riot in thing[s] attainable that it may not have leisure to go mad after thing[s] which are not" (*Letters*, vol. 1, 320). Keats seems to identify himself with Burns, or rather to see in Burns a destiny that could befall him as well[40]. Keats found himself in a poetic impasse: his "luxurious imagination" could not be deadened and restrained without affecting his inspiration, but at the same time he knew the risks which an uncontrolled imagination can lead to.

In November 1818 Keats praised a fresco by Carlo Lasinio he saw in a book of prints to George and Georgiana. The fresco is grotesque, "yet still making up a fine whole – even finer to me than more accomplish'd works – as there was left so much room for Imagination" (*Letters*, vol. 2, 19). Here Keats points out the important role of imagination in artistic reception as well as in production, which is what I am focusing on. In Book 2 of *Hyperion*, presumably written during the spring of 1819, Keats mentions again imagination as the faculty which allows to see things which are yet to come. Asia is "prophesying of her glory" (57) and she sees this glory "in her wide imagination" (58). His use of the verb 'prophesy' reiterates the non-rational, intuitive nature of the processes of imagination and it should also be remembered that prophecies are usually products of a heightened state of consciousness.

The need to curb imagination, however, had not been dismissed. It is hinted at again in the letter to George and Georgiana dated 21 April 1819, where, after copying out the text of *La Belle Dame Sans Merci*, he explains why the kisses she gives to the knight are four in the following terms: "why four because I wish to restrain the headlong impetuosity of my Muse – she would have fain said 'score' without hurting the rhyme – but we must temper the Imagination as the Critics say with Judgement" (*Letters*, vol. 2, 97). Although the tone of the passage is openly ironic and Keats attributes the opinion about the necessary restraint of imagination to the authority of some unnamed critics, he had already expressed himself in similar terms when writing to Hessey on 8 October 1818. In this letter, he affirms that, if previously he had written "independently *without Judgment*", from then on he will try to write "independently *& with Judgment*" (*Letters*, vol. 1, 374), an assertion that reveals how much seriousness underlies his joke about the Belle Dame's kisses. Furthermore, on 16 August 1820, in the letter which also contains his last meditation on poetic imagination, he gives the same

---

40 The misery of Burns's fate weighed so heavily on Keats's mind that the visit to his house did not arouse the expected inspiration. As he wrote in "This mortal body of a thousand days" (11 July 1818), "Fancy is dead and drunken at its goal" (8).

advice to Shelley by inviting him to furl the wings of his imagination and write with more discipline. Keats admits that this might seem odd talk for the author of *Endymion*, "whose mind was like a pack of scattered cards", but now "I am pick'd up and sorted to a pip. My Imagination is a Monastry and I am its Monk" (*Letters*, vol. 2, 323). Keats still represents his imagination with a metaphor associated with the sacred and the divine, as if to say that imagination is something sacred to the poet who must preserve it but also something that is not entirely of this world. The monastery, however, is also an image of a closed, secluded place, which implies a confinement and contrasts with the previous depiction of a free-wandering imagination. Ultimately, Keats seems to outline his own poetic development, and, if the cards of his mind have now been put in order, this newly acquired discipline does not mean a return to the Augustan poetic practice, as imagination is still the main poetic faculty and the poet himself the only authority.

This passage towards a new confidence – a confidence which is presumably partly feigned, as Keats is also trying to convey a certain idea of himself as a poet to his friend and rival Shelley – follows an important insight contained in *The Fall of Hyperion*. This second attempt to interpret the myth of Hyperion, which was begun in July 1819 and probably interrupted in December of the same year, opens with the following lines:

> Fanatics have their dreams, wherewith they weave
> A paradise for a sect, the savage too
> From forth the loftiest fashion of his sleep
> Guesses at Heaven; pity these have not
> Traced upon vellum or wild Indian leaf
> The shadows of melodious utterance.
> But bare of laurel they live, dream, and die;
> For Poesy alone can tell her dreams,
> With the fine spell of words alone can save
> Imagination from the sable charm
> And dumb enchantment. [...] (1–11)

Keats is here making a very clear statement about the nature of poetry and its relationship with imagination. As imagination is a faculty common to everyone, "every man whose soul is not a clod / Hath visions" (13–14), including savages, which leads to the need to define what makes a poet. The element that distinguishes poets from the rest of mankind is identified with the "utterance" (6) of the dream: "Poesy alone can tell her dreams" (8). While other men die without leaving traces of their dreams, poets are the only ones endowed with the ability to turn their visions into words – words which have the magic power of saving imagination. It has already been seen in "On Visiting the Tomb of Burns" that imagination can get diseased, but the nature of this disease has never been made explicit. Here it is described as a "sable charm / And dumb enchantment" (10–11), where 'dumb' specifically suggests an inability to speak (*OED:* 'destitute of the faculty of speech', 'not attended with vocal utterance', 'not emitting sound'). Poetic imagination gets sick when it indulges in visions without succeeding in expressing them through poetry. Two kinds of magic are contrasted here: the charm that enhances imagination in no more than fanatics' visions and the spell of poetic words which gives substance to the dreams produced by imagination. Thus, looking back to the famous 1817 letter to Bailey, it is poetry that guarantees the comparison between imagination and Adam's dream[41], as it is through poetic utterance that the dream is brought outside into the world and comes true.

The introduction of *The Fall of Hyperion* concludes with the doubt "Whether the dream now purposed to rehearse / Be poet's or fanatic's" (16–17), that is, whether the verbalisation of the dream in a poem will succeed. This process is more difficult than it might have appeared from these lines, and Keats is aware of it. As a matter of fact, *The Fall of Hyperion* itself, whose subtitle is precisely *A Dream*, is left unfinished, but its opening meditation and its fate can help shed new light on the passage in the verse letter to Reynolds which has already been analysed. Imagination has been seen to be depicted as in a liminal position, belonging to heaven but confined to earth. The opposition between these two spatial dimensions can be read at a further, metapoetic level. Imagination is related to heaven (see also *The Fall of Hyperion* 3, where the savage "Guesses at Heaven" through his dreams) not only because it deals with things which are not present, but also because it arises from the unconscious, which is usually metaphorically represented as otherworldly[42]. The divine nature of the unconscious derives from its being perceived by the conscious self as something other than itself and that eludes its control. On the other hand, consciousness, which dominates what we consider our ordinary experience of the world, is usually associated with earth.

Dreams and visions, the terms used to describe the products of imagination, originate in the unconscious, where a 'symmetrical logic' dominates. In order to write poetry, these visions need to be turned into words, but language is subjected to the laws of 'asymmetrical logic' due to its sequential nature. The two phrases are used by Matte Blanco to refer to the two different ways of being of the human mind: the asymmetrical mode is analytical, discriminating, and prevails

---

[41] It is precisely through the recurring of the relationship between imagination and dream that the two texts can be compared.

[42] Jung often insists on the divine or supernatural perception of the unconscious by human beings. While analysing the myth of Pandora, for instance, he points out that "The happenings in the other world are what takes place on the further side of consciousness, that is the unconscious" (*Psychological Types* 176).

in consciousness, while the symmetrical mode is all-inclusive, undifferentiating, and dominates the unconscious[43]. In order to prevent this impasse, in *The Fall of Hyperion* Keats focuses on the spell of poetic words, as magic is a sympathetic way of relating to the world. Yet language can never be entirely visionary if it wants to be understood by others. Every act of verbalisation implies the imposition of an order and a linearity that do not originally belong to the vision. This is the reason why, in the verse letter to Reynolds, Keats refers to two laws, that of heaven, i. e. of the vision, and that of earth, i. e. of language. Imagination produces poetry when a compromise between the two is achieved, but there is also the risk of the two levels becoming dissociated and imagination lost in an impasse. In the end, it is language itself that, in a sense, confines imagination.

2.2.2 Fancy

Keats does not draw a distinction between imagination and fancy as neatly as Coleridge. The dissimilar, almost complementary distribution of the two terms in letters and poetry, however, is rather significant and helps to understand how they are differently used. Imagination occurs in the letters far more often than in poetry and, in both cases, it is most of the time associated with poetic issues. As seen in the previous chapter, some of Keats's most important meditations about creativity revolve around imagination, especially when he is writing in prose. On the other hand, fancy is mentioned in the poems almost three times as often as imagination, which is partly due to the outer properties of the two words. While 'imagination' is polysyllabic and shows an evident Latin root, 'fancy' is a contraction of the Greek-derived 'fantasy', and may have been perceived as more indigenous and thus more suited to the new style of poetry that rejected the Latinate diction of Augustan poetry.

In the letters, however, 'fancy' is a rare occurrence, and it is contrasted with imagination only in the letter dated 8th October 1817 and mentioned above, where it seems to be the faculty that provides the actual materials of poetic composition – just as the sails materially allow the ship to proceed – but also a faculty that needs guidance. It is again associated with poetry in the letter to

---

43 See Matte Blanco, especially chapter 7. Furthermore, the asymmetrical mode and the symmetrical mode of being of the human mind can be related to what cognitive scholars now call convergent and divergent thinking, respectively. Both the asymmetrical mode and convergent thinking, in fact, focus on differences between things and are a feature of consciousness (Matte Blanco 96: "the essence of consciousness is to distinguish and to differentiate and that cannot be done with symmetrical relations alone"), whereas divergent thinking occurs in a state of defocused attention, when the mind is free to unconsciously wander and things coexist without contradiction according to the symmetrical mode.

Bailey about the truth of imagination, where Keats refers to "O Sorrow" as "a representation from the fancy of the probable mode of operating in these Matters" (*Letters*, vol. 1, 185), so that fancy corresponds to the general mode of poetry, as opposed to the discursive one of the letter. Keats defines fancy more precisely in a letter to Reynolds dated 11 July 1818: "Fancy is indeed less than a palpable reality, but it is greater than remembrance" (*Letters*, vol. 1, 325). This assertion is relevant for two reasons. First, it does not agree with Coleridge's definition of fancy as "a mode of Memory" (*Biographia Literaria*, vol. 1, 202), but depicts it as the ability to mentally represent something that has not been perceived, while memory is only the shadow of a perceived experience. Keats uses as example the imaginative power that arises during reading. Secondly, the products of fancy are placed below physical reality unlike those of imagination that are repeatedly said to be true, like Adam's dream. The fact that fancy is never associated with truth is one of the main differences between the two terms. In Book 1 of *Endymion* (1817), the shepherd relates his dream-encounters with Cynthia to his sister Peona and assures her that "these things are true" (850), even if revealed "beyond the shadow of a dream" (857), exactly as happened to Adam. His visionary experiences are something more than the "atomies / That buzz about our slumbers, like brain-flies, / Leaving us fancy-sick" (851–853), where fancy clearly stands for an inferior faculty that produces unreal dreams.

The only reference to a creative fancy is found in a letter to Rice dated 14 February 1820, where Keats writes about the flowers he has known since his infancy that "their shapes and coulours [*sic*] as are [*for* are as] new to me as if I had just created them with a superhuman fancy" (*Letters*, vol. 2, 260). Novelty is identified as a quality of the products of fancy, even if its creative power is here confined to a simile and, what is more, to the capability of a superhuman being. This set of images recalls one of the most relevant mentions of fancy in the poems, that is, at the end of the "Ode to Psyche" (1819), where Keats is describing the poetic mind during the act of creation through the metaphor of a fane with a garden. Fancy is "the gardener" (62) who presides and governs creation and whose function is so central that it seems to coincide with imagination. Yet Fancy must also "feign" (62) the flowers that will dress the sanctuary, i. e. provide the materials of the composition. 'Feign' is a verb that suggests the artificiality of creation; indeed, the flowers bred by Fancy are different from the natural ones, since they are never the same (63: "breeding flowers will never breed the same"). These flowers are always new because, being imaginative products, they are not modelled after nature and its finite variety of plants but, rather, spring from the endless abundance of fancy[44]. The insistence on novelty and profusion is, to

---

[44] Keats refers to the abundance of fancy's material in *Lamia* (1819) too, when he mentions

some degree, reminiscent of the Wordsworthian presentation of fancy, whereas the artful nature of its creation (the garden is a cultivated space in comparison with the wild sceneries described in the preceding lines) resembles Coleridge's mechanical fancy. "Ode to Psyche" is thus a perfect example of how imagination and fancy overlap in Keats's poetry, but without a complete identification.

There is still one more passage in the letters where the word 'fancy' appears, but possesses a more narrow, even if unique, sense. On 17 November 1819, while discussing with Taylor his future compositions, Keats wrote: "As the marvellous is the most enticing and the surest guarantee of harmonious numbers I have been endeavouring to persuade myself to untether Fancy and let her manage for herself" (*Letters*, vol. 2, 234). It has already been seen – and will be further seen – that the question whether to give free rein or not to the imaginative powers is rather crucial for Keats, but what is new here is that the free play of fancy is associated with the specific genre of the marvellous, as to say that unchecked fancy indulges in whimsical, unreal, fantastical images.

As far as poetry is concerned, another difference between imagination and fancy is the frequent presence of the latter in the very earliest writings of Keats. Even though fancy often recurs with the same ordinary meaning as imagination, that is, as the faculty of mentally representing something that is not real or present[45], it has also more significant uses. "How many bards gild the lapses of time", written in October 1816, is one of Keats's first descriptions of the creative process. He describes how the sensations first of other poems, then of nature accumulate in the mind of the artist and feed his fancy (2-3: "the food / Of my delighted fancy") in order to produce a work of art. Even though this process corresponds to the two kinds of imitation theorised in the 18th century and was soon to be rejected in favour of the Romantic spider poet who draws his materials from his inner vision, the idea that fancy can be 'fed' with outer sensations recurs quite often. In "Sleep and Poetry", written between October and December of the same year, Keats represents the successive stages of personal development, from unreflecting enjoyment in sensuous pleasure to the nobler understanding of the "Heart's affections". It is in the former that fancy plays a role by receiving these delightful sensations (104: "choose each pleasure that my fancy sees"), while, as already seen, imagination is present later in the same poem as the chief poetic faculty. In "I stood tip-toe upon a little hill" (Dec. 1816), Keats wonders what inspired the first poet to sing the myth of Narcissus and concludes that is was some perception of nature that impressed on his fancy

---

"rich gifts, unknown to any Muse, / Though Fancy's casket were unlocked to choose" (19-20).

45 In "To Hope" (Feb. 1815) and "To Charles Cowden Clarke" (Sept. 1816) fancy is associated with hope in the same terms as in the letter to Dilke dated 22 September 1819 (*Letters*, vol. 2, 178). See also "Time's Sea" (1818), 9-12, and "Why did I laugh tonight" (1819), 9-10.

(178: "Some fainter gleamings o'er his fancy shot"). The same ideas as those found in the two poems just named are to some extent further developed more than a year later in "Four seasons fill the measure of the year" (March 1818), where the progression of seasons is compared with the development of the human mind. The "lusty springs, when fancy clear / Takes in all beauty with an easy span" (3-4) again shows a receptive fancy that is, however, inferior to imagination. Summer can, in fact, be interpreted as the period of imagination which concentrates only on inner materials, as the outer sensorial impressions gathered by fancy are now part of the human mind[46], which "by such dreaming" (7) allows the man to come "His nearest unto heaven"[47]. The man needs then to tether his imagination in autumn, "when his wings / He furleth close", which is precisely the same metaphor used two years later in the letter to Shelley quoted above. All these poems insist on the idea of a perceptive fancy that recalls one of the two natures of imagination, more precisely, that which seizes beauty that already exists.

In addition, the metaphors of free wandering and tethering are applied to fancy as well as to imagination, so that the meanings of these two terms are again brought together. In "Fill for me a brimming bowl", written in August 1814, the epithet for fancy is already "wandering" (12), as if to say that Keats soon becomes aware of its non-linear, divergent functioning. On the idea of a roaming fancy Keats bases his whole "Fancy", the rondeau devoted to this faculty, probably written in December 1818. Throughout the poem he repeatedly invites the reader to "Break the mesh / Of the Fancy's silken lash" (89-90) and to "let winged Fancy wander" (6). Like imagination, fancy is here the faculty of making present things that are not and its action is precisely the same, yet overturned, as happens with imagination in the verse letter to Reynolds. While there imagination mined the present state of summer happiness by evoking a wintry gloom, here fancy is able to bring "in spite of frost, / Beauties that the earth hath lost" (29-30). It works according to a symmetrical mode, as it brings about the coexistence of pleasures belonging to every season by annihilating the succession of time that is possible only in the asymmetrical mode of consciousness[48].

---

46 See the copy of the poem in the letter to Bailey dated 13 March 1818: "He chews the honied cud of fair spring thoughts, / Till, in his Soul dissolv'd they come to be / Part of himself" (6-8).
47 It has been seen in the previous chapter how this set of terms is usually associated with imagination.
48 Matte Blanco asserts that time, as it is a succession of distinct instants, is not possible in the symmetrical mode, which considers every relation symmetrical, so that 'x comes after y' is equivalent to 'y comes after x'. The principle of symmetry is identified by Matte Blanco as the second principle of the system of the Unconscious (38), and he asserts that "the absence of temporal process is an inevitable consequence of the second principle, because the existence of a succession of moments requires a serial ordination; and if asymmetrical relations are barred, according to the symbolic logic there can be no such ordination" (42).

Fancy and imagination overlap, partly because of their occurring in states of heightened consciousness and activation of visionary powers. In Book 2 of *Endymion* (1817), the "Brain-sick shepherd prince" (43) has been "wandering in uncertain ways" (48) before his fancy is snared (57) and he sees "strange things" (62) that make him wonder. Likewise, in "The Eve of St. Agnes" (Jan.-Feb. 1819), fancy is the faculty that allows Madeline, who is "Hoodwinked with fairy fancy" (70), to experience the supernatural vision of St. Agnes: "Pensive awhile she dreams awake, and sees, / In fancy, fair St. Agnes in her bed, / But dares not look behind, or all the charm is fled" (232–234). This condition of wakeful dreaming is a visionary state typical of Keats[49].

2.2.3 Invention

The term 'invention' derives from the *inventio* of Classical rhetoric, i.e. the discovery of sources and materials upon which to build an oration. In the passage of the letter to Bailey quoted above, dated 8 October 1817, it seems to refer to the faculty of providing narrative incidents, trains of events and set of images to fill out the main conception of the poem – in this case *Endymion* –, but it also seems to be evaluated above the other two poetic faculties. This unusual hierarchy is not found anywhere else in the corpus of Keats's letters, where imagination is always present as the chief poetic power, and it is thus clearly applied only to long narrative poems. Keats insists that *Endymion* must be "a trial of my Imagination and chiefly of my invention which is a rare thing indeed – by which I must make 4000 Lines of one bare circumstance and fill them with Poetry" (*Letters*, vol. 1, 169–170). In order to succeed in this demanding literary enterprise, Keats needs the conscious powers of invention, which had lately been neglected by the Romantics, and for once places it even above imagination.

That invention is a conscious, rational faculty is confirmed by the other two mentions of the term in Keats's letters. The term 'invention', in fact, never occurs in the poems, and, even in prose, it is related to poetic composition only in the passage already cited, which reinforces the idea that Keats does not build his poetic conception on it. In a letter to Bailey dated 13 March 1818, Keats tries to find some excuse for not visiting him while in Oxford and writes: "I have been rubbing up my invention; trying several sleights" (*Letters*, vol. 1, 241), but, since nothing would do, he finally tells Bailey the true reason. After almost two years,

---

49 The most two famous references are in "Ode to Psyche" (5–6) and in "Ode to a Nightingale" (79–80), where fancy represents the illusory aspect, i.e. the limitations, of the imaginative, sympathetic identification of the poetic persona with the nightingale (73–74: "The fancy cannot cheat so well / As she is famed to do, deceiving elf").

on 13 January 1820, he writes to his sister-in-law Georgiana: "Now I have been sitting here a half hour with my invention at work to say something about your Mother or Charles or Henry but it is in vain – I know not what to say" (*Letters*, vol. 2, 242). In both cases, invention appears to be a deliberate exertion of the intellect to find something to say through an ingenious effort of rational thinking. Likewise, as far as *Endymion* is concerned, it stands as the ability to skilfully expand the main circumstance of the myth thanks to embellishments and a plot full of incidents. What is significant here is that, in order to make his literary debut, Keats chose a genre that was eccentric with respect to the Romantic canon and, as a result, he had to rediscover an ability that the Romantics ignored because of their predilection for lyrical poetry. However, the tension between conformity to Romantic diction and obedience to his personal vision was never resolved, as is proven by the fact that, although he continued to attempt long narrative poems (*Hyperion* 1820, *Lamia* 1820, *The Fall of Hyperion* 1856), his best-known poetic achievements belong to the typically Romantic genre of the ode.

2.2.4 Beauty

Beauty is another key term in Keats's poetic conception and some of its most pertinent aspects have already been mentioned talking of imagination. First of all, the sense of beauty is identified with one of the main qualities of the modern artist, in opposition to the Augustans, who were so concentrated on their laws and conventions that they did not seem to realise that "Beauty was awake" ("Sleep and Poetry" 192). Beauty must be the aim and the driving force of every act of creation, and Keats himself often ascribes his poetic vocation to his love of beauty[50]. On 9 April 1818, he wrote to Reynolds that he had never written a single line of poetry giving the slightest consideration to the public, as he feels a certain humility only towards "the eternal Being, the Principle of Beauty, – and the Memory of great Men" (*Letters*, vol. 1, 266), while, in a letter to Woodhouse dated 27 October 1818, he goes so far as to say: "I feel assured I should write from the mere yearning and fondness I have for the Beautiful even if my night's labours should be burnt every morning and no eye ever shine upon them" (*Letters*, vol. 1, 388).

The reason for this centrality of beauty in art can be found in a letter to George and Tom which dates back to 21 December 1817, where Keats relates his impressions about Benjamin West's *Death on the Pale Horse* (1817). Keats complains that the painting has "nothing to be intense upon; no women one feels

---

50 For Keats's insistence on his love of beauty, see also *Letters*, vol. 1, 373 and 404.

mad to kiss; no face swelling into reality" and goes on to assert that "The excellence of every Art is its intensity, capable of making all disagreeables [*sic*] evaporate, from their being in close relationship with Beauty & Truth" (*Letters*, vol. 1, 192)[51]. This passage carries clear echoes of the letter to Bailey about the authenticity of imagination, as Keats was meditating on the same concepts, here explicitly applied to art. Excellent art is based on the fundamental relationship between beauty and truth[52]. As Adam dreams of Eve, and wakes to find his dream come true in the outer world, so Keats expects something to come out of the painting and strike him with its reality, but this can happen only through the mediation of the intensity of emotional involvement. Only if the observer wants to kiss a face, can that face become real. As already seen, passions guarantee the truth of imagination because they create beauty.

This leads to another main characteristic of beauty, that is, its duality. According to Keats, beauty is both an object of creation and of perception. On one hand, passions are "creative of essential Beauty" (*Letters*, vol. 1, 184), but, on the other, beauty is referred to in the same letter as something to be 'seized', i.e. perceived. Furthermore, the perception of beauty is placed at the end of "the labyrinthian path to eminence in Art" in a letter to Haydon dated 8 April 1818, where Keats describes this path in terms of "The innumerable compositions and decompositions which take place between the intellect and its thousand materials before it arrives at that trembling delicate and snail-horn perception of Beauty – I know not you[r] many havens of intenseness" (*Letters*, vol. 1, 264– 265). Keats writes "you[r]" because he is explicitly referring to painting, but the idea of a non-linear creative development can presumably be applied to every art, as poetic imagination too is said to go into labyrinths in "Sleep and Poetry". The metaphor of the snail is drawn from *Venus and Adonis* (1593), where Shakespeare refers to snails' habit of stretching out their horns and shrinking them back into their shell when they are hit[53]. Likewise, Keats seems to hint at a perception of beauty that is only momentary, as it is followed by a necessary retreat of the artist into his inner being.

---

51 For the use of the chemical metaphor of evaporation, see Goellnicht 55–58.
52 The equivalence between beauty and truth is expressed in the famous but debatable conclusion of "Ode on a Grecian Urn" too: "Beauty is truth, truth beauty' – that is all / Ye know on earth, and all ye need to know" (49–50).
53 "Or as the snail, whose tender horns being hit, / Shrinks backward in his shelly cave with pain, / And there all smother'd up in shade doth sit, / Long after fearing to creep forth again" (*Venus and Adonis* 1033–1036).

2.2.5 Negative Capability

In the same letter dealing with West's *Death on the Pale Horse*, Keats presents his theory about the quality that makes a man of achievement in literature and uses for the first and only time his famous phrase 'negative capability', that is, "when man is capable of being in uncertainties, Mysteries, doubts, without any irritable reaching after fact & reason" (*Letters*, vol. 1, 193). Shakespeare possessed this quality in the highest measure, whereas Coleridge lacks it due to his interest in German idealistic philosophy and his desire to discover ultimate truths through reason. He is "incapable of remaining content with half knowledge" (*Letters*, vol. 1, 194), whereas, in a great poet, the sense of beauty should obliterate every other consideration. Just as Coleridge does not possess Negative Capability, not even the other great Romantic poet possesses it. In an important letter to Richard Woodhouse dated 27 October 1818, Wordsworth is considered to be an "egotistical sublime" kind of poet, who does not belong to the true poetical character because of his too self-centred poems and, therefore, of what Keats calls his egotism. Here Keats is distancing himself from the contemporary poet who had the deepest influence on him. Nevertheless, this distancing never became definitive, as Keats continued to hold an ambivalent attitude towards his Romantic models. At the beginning of his career, Keats had looked up to Wordsworth as the initiator of the modern way of writing poetry, and considered *The Excursion* among the "three things superior in the modern world" (*Letters*, vol. 1, 204) as well as a work of genius[54]. He now defines the main attribute of poetic genius in very different terms:

> As to the poetical Character itself, (I mean that sort of which, if I am any thing, I am a Member; that sort distinguished from the wordsworthian or egotistical sublime; which is a thing per se and stands alone) it is not itself – it has no self – it is every thing and nothing – It has no character [...] A Poet is the most unpoetical of any thing in existence; because he has no Identity – he is continually in for – and filling some other Body – The Sun, the Moon, the Sea and Men and Women who are creatures of impulse are poetical and have about them an unchangeable attribute – the poet has none (*Letters*, vol. 1, 386–387).

The true poetic character has no identity in itself, but is capable of participating in that of the objects of its own compositions. Negative capability, which Keats initially derived from his medical studies and from Hazlitt's idea of disinterestedness, can be considered as a different, perhaps more extreme appli-

---

[54] Keats repeatedly uses the word 'genius' in the modern Romantic sense (see *Letters*, vol. 1, 184, 205 and 386).

cation of the Romantic notion of sympathy[55]. It involves a going out of oneself (etymologically 'ecstasy') and an identification with another being that blurs the boundaries between self and other. The poet is defined through his lack of autonomous, stable identity, that is, through his power to go beyond himself. He is as much "filling", as Keats puts it, as filled, so that this concept too possesses a fundamental duality. The condition of the poet is one of self-forgetfulness and imaginative openness that allows him to experience what another feels. The role of imagination in the experience of negative capability is made explicit in a letter written in October 1818, where Keats asserts: "I feel more and more every day, as my imagination strengthens, that I do not live in this world alone but in a thousand worlds" (*Letters*, vol. 1, 403). He shouts with Achilles at Troy, he is with Theocritus in the vales of Sicily, or he throws his "whole being" into Troilus.

The fact that negative capability acts upon the poet through imagination points out another difference between Keats's and Coleridge's conceptions of imagination. Coleridge sees imagination as a power unifying the opposites; conversely, Keats expects a poet to be able to stand contradictions and be open to mystery. Metaphorically, the true poet bears a closer resemblance to the flower than the bee and delights more in passivity. He should "not therefore go hurrying about and collecting honey-bee like, buzzing here and there impatiently from a knowledge of what is to be arrived at; but [...] open [his] leaves like a flower and be passive and receptive" (*Letters*, vol. 1, 232). The most precious resource for a selfless poet cannot be other than receptiveness. In the end, through his conception of negative capability, Keats seems to reject the exaggerated stress laid on subjectivity by Romanticism in favour of a new predominance of the object that will influence some of the most important artists of Modernism, such as Yeats and Eliot[56].

2.2.6 Spontaneous growth *vs* deliberate creation

It has already been seen that Keats considered imagination as an unconscious, spontaneous faculty and that in "Ode to Psyche", for instance, he describes an outburst of inspiration as occurring in a condition of mental wandering and almost heightened consciousness[57]. In other passages in his letters, he even refers to impressions of writing at random, as if he followed some inexplicable impulse beyond his understanding, yet the results turned out to make perfect

---

55 See Caldwell 36–37 and Goellnicht 153–156 for the relations between negative capability, Hazlitt and sympathy in medicine.
56 See Li, chapter 4, for an analysis of the Modernist heritage of negative capability.
57 The poetic persona is actually unsure whether he is dreaming or conscious: "Surely I dreamt today, or did I see / The wingèd Psyche with awakened eyes?" (5–6).

sense when later examined. In a letter to Haydon dated 10 May 1817, he admitted: "I remember your saying that you had notions of a good Genius presiding over you – I have of late had the same thought for things which [I] do half *at Random* [italics added] are afterwards confirmed by my judgement in a dozen features of Propriety" (*Letters*, vol. 1, 142), while two years later he wrote to George and Georgiana: "I am however young writing *at random* [italics added] – straining at particles of light in the midst of a great darkness – without knowing the bearing of any one assertion of any one opinion" (*Letters*, vol. 2, 80). Keats seems to agree with the Romantics that inspiration springs from the unconscious and works in the artist independently of his will and conscious control. As he wrote in the letter to Hessey of 8 October 1818, "The Genius of Poetry must work out its own salvation in a man: It cannot be matured by law & precept, but by sensation & watchfulness in itself – That which is creative must create itself" (*Letters*, vol. 1, 374). Poetry is something that grows spontaneously within the artist and follows no other rules than its own. The most appropriate metaphor is precisely that of natural growth, so much so that Keats argues that "if Poetry comes not as naturally as the leaves to a tree it had better not come at all" (*Letters*, vol. 1, 238–239).

This comparison between artistic creation and springing leaves dates back to the first months of 1818, yet over time Keats developed also a different model of poetic composition as he revaluated the importance of study and discipline to attain knowledge and – what is more important – in poetic practice. In the same letter to Hessey about the autonomy of the "Genius of Poetry", Keats points to a new direction in his development as an author. Not only does he wish to write independently, that is, according to his personal inclination, but he wishes to write "independently & *with judgment*" (*Letters*, vol. 1, 374), whereas previously he had lacked the latter. 'Judgment' suggests the idea of a conscious, discerning faculty that leads to a deliberate creation controlled by the will of the artist. As already seen, Keats suggests these same control and discipline to Shelley and in September 1819 he wrote to George and Georgiana that he longed to substitute the "fever" writing verses leaves behind with "a more thoughtful and quiet power" (*Letters*, vol. 2, 209). The term 'thoughtful' suggests a revaluation of the rational faculty too.

As a matter of fact, Keats's views on reason and rational thinking – in his terms 'Thought' – are more complex than what has been considered so far, and are apparently contradictory. In line with common Romantic beliefs, Keats usually rejects thought as a means of acquiring truth in favour of imagination and sensation[58], since he has "never yet been able to perceive how any thing can

---

58 Sensations stand for an unmediated perception of the world and this 18th-century sensationalist approach is often hinted at besides the modern intuitive one based on imagination.

be known for truth by consequitive reasoning" (*Letters*, vol. 1, 185). Nevertheless, at a certain point, he happens to see rationally-acquired knowledge as a necessary support to sensations, as the wings to a flying bird[59], and he sometimes plans to devote his years to "continual drinking of knowledge" through "application study and thought" (*Letters*, vol. 1, 271), a project that is quite far from Romantic principles and is more reminiscent of rationalism. Keats even goes on to say: "I have been hovering for some time between an exquisite sense of the luxurious and a love for Philosophy – were I calculated for the former I should be glad – but as I am not I shall turn all my soul to the latter" (*ibidem*). Actually, this is only partly true. Keats wrote these words on 24 April 1818, but he continued to hover between these two opposites all his life.

Furthermore, these two different ways of composing poetry – the unconscious, spontaneous, inspired one led by imagination, and the conscious, intentional one controlled by the will and the judgement – coexist as different moments of the same creative process in Woodhouse's recollection of Keats's words about his own working practice: "My judgement, (he says,) is as active while I am actually writing as my imagination. In fact, all my faculties are strongly excited, & in their full play – And shall I afterwards, when my imagination is idle, & the heat in which I wrote, has gone off, sit down coldly to criticise when in possession of only one faculty, what I have written when almost inspired" (*Keats Circle*, vol. 1, 128–129). Keats's assertion is interesting as well as contradictory. In fact, he initially acknowledges an interplay between his mental faculties during the act of creation, but then he seems to limit the rational component to a simple revision, so that the poem seems to "come by chance or magic[60] – to be as it were something given to him" (129). However, as previously hinted, writing cannot occur only under the guidance of the divergent imagination – Keats himself says "*almost* [italics added] inspired" –, since verbalisation implies the activation of convergent processes as well. Ultimately, this issue is not unrelated to that of genre, as the model of a conscious, deliberate creation seems to be related to the notion of invention and to be almost inevitable when the composition of narrative poems is taken into account. In fact, just as a short lyric poem can be said to be written in a sudden outburst of

---

See, for instance, "axioms in philosophy are not axioms until they are proved upon our pulses" (*Letters*, vol. 1, 279) and "Nothing ever becomes real till it is experienced" (*Letters*, vol. 2, 81).

59 "The difference of high Sensations with and without knowledge appears to me this – in the letter case we are falling continually ten thousand fathoms deep and being blown up again without wings and with all [the] horror of a <Case> bare shouldered Creature – in the former case, our shoulders are fledge<d>, and we go thro' the same air and space without fear" (*Letters*, vol. 1, 277).

60 The link between magic and the spontaneity of Romantic poetic creation will turn out to be extremely important during the analysis of serpent symbolism.

inspiration⁶¹, a long poem necessarily needs more careful planning and constant discipline, as Keats's descriptions of his daily work on his narrative poems clearly show.

---

61 See Brown's narration of the composition of "Ode to a Nightingale", which is, however, probably an invention conforming to Romantic stereotypes: "In the spring of 1819 a nightingale had built her nest near my house. Keats felt a tranquil and continual joy in her song; and one morning he took his chair from the breakfast-table to the grass-plot under a plum-tree, where he sat for two or three hours. When he came into the house, I perceived he had some scraps of paper in his hand, and these he was quietly thrusting behind the books. On inquiry, I found those scraps, four or five in number, contained his poetic feelings on the song of the nightingale" (*Keats Circle*, vol. 2, 65).

3. Keats's serpents

3.1 Physical characteristics

In order to understand what the serpent represents in Keats's poetry, I will now refer to its physical characteristics in comparison with those identified and interpreted by Jung when analysing the archetypal significance of the snake. My approach, however, will adopt a slightly different point of view, since I consider the serpent not as a universal archetype belonging to the collective unconscious of all human beings as such[62] but as a 'living symbol' that is culturally determined and defined on an intersubjective, instead of universal, basis. This means that what Jung observes about the serpent can be applied to Keats because he finds an analogous image of this animal in culture, i.e. manly in literary tradition and folklore, and this image is culturally shaped so that it is suited to convey what he is aiming to express. On the other hand, it is presumably from his studies in biology and physiology[63] that he derives the precise knowledge of the physical characteristics of the snake, on which its culturally signifying attributes strictly depend.

First of all, the serpent is an animal and should be considered as part of a wider theriomorphic symbolism that Jung always associates with the unconscious. As Jung points out in *Aion* (1951), "Theriomorphic symbols are very common in dreams and other manifestations of the unconscious. They express the psychic level of the content in question; that is to say, such contents are at a stage of unconsciousness that it is as far from the human consciousness as the

---

62 "The contents of the personal unconscious are chiefly the *feeling-toned complexes*, as they are called; they constitute the personal and private side of psychic life. The contents of the collective unconscious, on the other hand, are known as *archetypes*" (Jung, *The Archetypes and the Collective Unconscious* 4).
63 For an overview of the medical treatises about snakes written between the end of the 18th century and the beginning of the 19th and of the common beliefs of the time, see De Almeida (184–187). Among the medical practitioners who published research about poisonous snakes there was Astley Cooper, whose lectures Keats attended at Guy's Hospital.

psyche of an animal" (186). Being devoid of human self-awareness and rational potential as well as being dominated by instincts, animals represent the unconscious, instinctual nature of the psyche, which is perceived by the conscious human mind as something other than itself to the same extent as animals are remote from humans. In the same passage in *Aion*, however, Jung suggests the idea that different kinds of animals indicate different "degree[s] of unconsciousness" (168), depending on how distant that animal is considered to be from human standards and on its different traits. Thus, each animal is associated with different aspects of the unconscious[64]. I will now focus on the characteristics of the snake which emerge throughout Jung's works and that have been singled out by his disciple Barbara Hannah in her interesting study *The Archetypal Symbolism of Animals* in order to see whether and how Keats refers to them in his poetry and to identify what elements of the unconscious snakes are associated with.

According to Jung, the serpent is "an excellent symbol for the unconscious, perfectly expressing the latter's sudden and unexpected manifestations" (Jung, *Symbols of Transformation* 374). This sentence already contains an important specification: the serpent is related not so much to the unconscious in its entirety as to the abrupt, unpredictable way its contents arise to the threshold of consciousness[65]. Snakes, indeed, react to stimuli in an unmediated way without resorting to the discriminating power of the brain, which is far less developed in them than in mammals or birds. As a consequence, their reactions depend entirely on the sympathetic nervous system[66] and they appear to be purely instinctual creatures. This leads to the remarkable rapidity of snakes and the

---

64 In *Aion*, for instance, Jung identifies the "monstrous, warlike lamb" with a "shadow-figure" (106) in opposition to the sacrificial lamb and the jellyfish with "our untamed and apparently untameable propensities" (135) that burn and defile the body. Moreover, he asserts that cold-blooded animals, such as dragons, crocodiles, or fish, can substitute the serpent in representing "the dark, chthonic world of instinct" (244). In *The Archetypes and the Collective Unconscious*, however, Jung distinguishes between the serpent and the fish: "As a rule the snake personifies the unconscious, whereas the fish usually represents one of its contents [...] [they] correspond to two different stages of development, the snake representing a more primitive and more instinctual state than the fish" (370). Moreover, the horse can be interpreted as the faculty of intuition (*The Archetypes and the Collective Unconscious* 233), while "birds, as aerial beings, are well-known spirit symbols" (334). Many other examples of theriomorphic symbolism could be mentioned, but it is important to note that, even if each animal represents different aspects of the unconscious due to its own characteristics, it is never a matter of univocal correspondence.
65 "As Jung points out, snakes are often symbols for psychic happenings or experiences that suddenly dart out of the unconscious and have frightening or redeeming effect" (Hannah 153). The axiological ambivalence of the serpent is a main point on which I will return later.
66 See Hannah 155 and Jung, *Symbols of Transformation* 374 ("Among the Gnostics it was regarded as an emblem of the brain-stem and spinal cord, as is consistent with its predominantly reflex psyche").

impossibility of predicting their movements, which are determined solely by reflex principles. In Keats's poems, the serpents disappear as instantaneously as they appear. In Book 3 of *Endymion* (1817), for instance, after some moments of "appalling silence" (327), the herd of Circe's victims suddenly forms the shape of Python in the sky and immediately vanishes[67], while at the end of *Lamia* the serpent-woman similarly disappears with a scream (Lamia II 306: "with a frightful scream she vanished"). However, Lamia's ability to vanish and reappear in unexpected places marks her movements even before the ending, for instance after her metamorphosis (*Lamia* I 165–166: "she / Melted and disappeared as suddenly" and 173: "she fled into the valley"), or before the nuptial ceremony (II 142: "she faded at self-will"). The effect of sudden disappearance is confirmed by a strong phonosymbolism. In fact, these lines from *Lamia* present a concentration of voiceless fricatives[68] that work onomatopoeically[69], as they mimetically reproduce the swish of a sneaking movement. As a result, Lamia's vanishing ability is conveyed on a phonemic level in addition to the semantic one.

This extreme speed of movement is also suggested by the skeletal and muscular construction of the snake, which allows it to move in every direction except backwards. Rapidity and extraordinary mobility are, thus, linked[70] but should not be confused. At times, its movements can also be very slow, as proved by the passage in *Hyperion* where a serpent-like agony passes through the Titan's limbs "Making slow way" (262). The focus is here on the snake's "vast and muscular" (261) body and on its "gradual" (258) progression through Hyperion. The verb used to describe its motion is 'creep' (258: "crept"), i.e. 'to move with the body prone and close to the ground, as a short-legged reptile, an insect, a quadruped moving stealthily' (*OED*), which is typically associated with reptiles (*OED*: 'originally, creeping or crawling animals') but not specifically with serpents, as it does not exclude the use of paws[71]. As a matter of fact, Keats never describes the

---

67 "For the whole herd, as by a whirlwind writhen, / Went through the dismal air like one huge Python / Antagonizing Boreas – and so vanished" (*Endymion* III 529–531).
68 Voiceless fricatives are underlined in the following lines: "she / Melted and disappeared as suddenly" (*Lamia* I 165–166); "she fled into the valley" (173); "she faded at self-will" (II 142); "with a frightful scream she vanished" (306). It is important to note that, in these lines, voiceless fricatives are often placed at the beginning of words, so that they are further emphasised.
69 I refer to Hrushovski's definition of onomatopoeia: "a word (or a group of words) in which a *part* of the sound is, in some way, equivalent to a *part* (or an aspect, or a metonymy) of the designation, if that part designates a sound in nature" (46).
70 "The skeletal and muscular construction is such that they can move in every direction except backward, swift silent motion being characteristic of the snake. It appears suddenly and unexpectedly, which corresponds to our own experience of things in the unconscious and to the appearance of serpents in visions, and so on" (Hannah 160).
71 Keats himself uses the verb 'creep' in reference to animals endowed with paws, such as

movement of snakes exactly in terms of slithering, but prefers a verb like 'creep', which conveys the idea of moving slowly and stealthy, as if to elude observation, or 'sprawl', which suggests a spreading out in an untidy or irregular way. In the first scene of the fifth act of *Otho the Great*, Auranthe exclaims: "A snake, / A scorpion, sprawling on the first gold step, / Conducting to the throne high canopied" (14–16). Furthermore, in Book 3 of *Endymion*, 'serpent' is turned into a verb and applied to the men Circe turned into animals: "And all around her shapes, wizard and brute, / Laughing, and wailing, grovelling, serpenting, / Showing tooth, tusk, and venom-bag, and sting! / Oh, such deformities!" (500–503). These lines are a perfect portrayal of the "swarming, wriggling, or chaotic movement" (Durand 72) that, according to Durand, is one of the main attributes of dysphoric animality in archetypal imagery. Disorganised animation (see again 'sprawl') distinguishes animals – in this specific case serpents – as something fleetingly dynamic, which eludes the human grasp ('creep' implies not being seen) and constantly escapes us through its unexpected movements.

All these features can be easily applied to the manifestations of the unconscious, which are equally unpredictable, spontaneous, beyond our control and seemingly chaotic, as they respond to other laws than those of consciousness (what is called 'symmetrical logic' as opposed to 'asymmetrical logic'). This is also the reason why, as already seen, the unconscious is perceived by the conscious mind as something 'other' than itself. A perfect correspondence with the serpent can be found again here, as this animal "symbolizes to the human being the 'totally other'" (Hannah 156). Among animals, the serpent is, in fact, the most removed one from man, partly due to the attributes that have just been analysed, partly to some others that emerge from the following significant passages in *Aion*: "the snake does in fact symbolize 'cold-blooded', inhuman contents [...] in a word, the extra-human quality in man" (186) and "[the serpent] appears spontaneously or comes as a surprise; it fascinates; its glance is staring, fixed, unrelated; its blood cold, and it is a stranger to man" (188). In *Symbols of Transformation*, Jung insists that "the serpent is a cold-blooded creature, unconscious and unrelated" (374).

Being cold-blooded is constantly linked with the serpent's estrangement from man. The serpent is basically cold, with a body temperature that has always been metaphorically associated with a certain lack of affect and humanity. Nonetheless, snakes depend more than other animals on external heat, so that they can be seen as unifying the two opposites[72], which is a recurring theme when serpent symbolism is under discussion. Keats refers, in particular, to the tem-

---

monkeys in "When they were come unto the Fairy's court" (90: "And then the thievish monkeys down would creep").

72 See Hannah 155.

perature of a serpent when he depicts Lamia's metamorphosis into a woman in Book 1. The description abounds in terms belonging to the isotopy of heat: even her eyes are "hot" (150) and "with lid-lashes all sear, / Flashed phosphor and sharp sparks, without one cooling tear" (150-151), while the colours of her skin are "all inflamed" (152) and substituted by a "volcanian yellow" (155), which is compared with "the lava" that "ravishes the mead" (157). The sudden heat significantly marks her transformation from snake to human being, from a cold-blooded to a warm-blooded being. Again, phonosymbolism reinforces the semantic meaning of the passage. The voiceless palate-alveolar sibilant fricative /ʃ/ recurs in line 150[73] and has a twofold effect. On one hand, it onomatopoeically recalls the sizzle of phosphor and burning substances. On the other, it is produced by channelling the sound along the palate until it reaches with the nearly clenched teeth and it is distinguished by audible friction, as the air is forced through a constricted passage. Its own articulation can thus be compared with the act of rubbing[74], which generates heat. Lamia's temperature increases again in Book 2, where, when perceiving Lycius's cruelty, "She burnt, she loved the tyranny" (81). Heat is associated with a form of behaviour that Keats considers to be specifically womanly[75] and indeed it immediately follows a denial of Lamia's serpent nature[76].

'Unrelated' is another key adjective that Jung regularly employs in referring to serpents. If it is true that human beings can enter into relation with other animals, even though they represent some kind of otherness as well, we never become truly familiar with a snake, nor can it ever be domesticated or made to serve our purposes[77]. Most of the time, serpents simply do not seem to be aware of humans, and, even if they are, they apparently do not care. What prevents any possibility of true contact is precisely this lack of interest that the serpent manifests towards human beings and, what is more, its lack of empathy, which

---

73 "with lid-la<u>sh</u>es all sear, / Fla<u>sh</u>ed phosphor and <u>sh</u>arp sparks" (*Lamia* I 150).
74 More in general, 'fricative' comes from the Latin 'fricare', which means precisely 'to rub', as the articulation of fricatives is produced through a constriction in the oral cavity that produces a friction in phonation. In fact, other fricatives recur in the lines as well: "wi<u>th</u> lid-lashe<u>s</u> all <u>s</u>ear, / <u>F</u>lashed <u>ph</u>os<u>ph</u>or and sharp spark<u>s</u>, wi<u>th</u>out one cooling tear" (*Lamia* I 150-151).
75 See Keats's comment recorded in Woodhouse's letter to Taylor dated 19, 20 September 1819: "Women love to be forced to do a thing, by a fine fellow – *such as this*" (*Keats Circle*, vol. 1, 93).
76 "The serpent – ha, the serpent! Certes, she / Was none" (*Lamia* II 80-81).
77 "But with the domestic animals we are dealing with instincts that can be domesticated and which, to a great extent, can be tamed and even used for our own purposes [...]. But when it comes to such creatures as the serpent, all efforts at domestication come to an end. A serpent can never be made to serve our purposes, and this may be one of the reasons why it figures so universally in symbolizing what is foreign, strange, and far removed from man" (Hannah 130).

seems to distinguish cold-blooded animals from warm-blooded ones[78]. For instance, Lamia most clearly reveals her predatory – and thus serpent-like – nature when she does not manifest "any show / Of sorrow for her tender favourite's woe" (290-291), that is, when she does not feel any sympathy for Lycius's sufferings.

However, Keats favours another way of displaying the otherness of the serpent, that is, through the isotopy of the supernatural. In Keats's poetry, snakes are often unearthly creatures or associated with some of them. Besides being half-woman and half-serpent, Lamia is presented as a fairy: her blood is "elfin" (*Lamia* I 147), she awaits Lycius "so fairily / By the wayside" (I 200-201) and her song is "too sweet for earthly lyres" (I 299). The narrator compares her to "some penanced lady elf, / Some demon's mistress, or the demon's self" (I, 55-56), while Lycius admits that he has always thought her "Not mortal, but of heavenly progeny" (II, 87). In addition, these last two quotes effectively express the duality of supernaturalness, which ranges from demoniacal to heavenly. In "Song of Four Fairies", "Adder-eyed Dusketha" (68) is a serpent-like fairy as well as spirit of the earth, while the Fury Alecto has snakes for hair (*Endymion* II 875), and a serpent is the attribute of the Titan Iapetus in Book 2 of *Hyperion* (44-48). Lastly, snakes are associated with Circe, who is a nymph endowed with magical powers, in Book 3 of *Endymion*, where the products of her spells are compared with the mythological Python[79] (530), and her true nature is revealed to Glaucus through the prodigious apparition of a fire in the shape of a snake's eye (494). As already seen when dealing with Keats's conception of creativity, something is symbolically imagined to belong to another world when it happens in the reign of the unconscious, as the latter seems to be 'totally other' from the standpoint of ordinary – i.e. conscious – life, just like the divine[80] or, in Keats's non-religious worldview, the supernatural from the standpoint of ordinary – i.e. earthly – life.

Thus, the serpent symbolises the totally extra-human in both senses of subhuman – as it is a purely instinctual, unrelated, unempathic animal – and of superhuman – as it is endowed with supernatural properties. Since imagination

---

78 "Hagenbeck, the famous connoisseur of animals, said that you can establish a physical rapport with practically all animals until one comes to snakes, alligators and such creatures, and there it comes to an end […]. Warm-blooded animals have an idea of man; they are either friendly, or they avoid him and his habitations because they dislike or are afraid of him. But snakes are absolutely heedless. So we must assume that cold-blooded animals have an entirely different kind of psychology – one could say none, but that is a little arbitrary. These old-blooded relics are in a way uncanny powers, because they symbolize the fundamental factor of our instinctive life" (Jung, *Dream Analysis* 645).
79 As a matter of fact, the huge Python itself is something more than a natural snake.
80 "When I speak of the divine as 'totally other,' I mean that, from a standpoint of ordinary life, it seems to be the 'totally other'" (Hannah 154).

has already been said to be depicted by Keats as belonging to another world[81] too, a comparison between the two can now be attempted. The unexpected apparitions and sudden movements of snakes symbolise the unpredictable way the contents of the unconscious reach the conscious level. Likewise, according to Keats and the Romantics, imagination arises spontaneously from the unconscious and cannot be exerted through the will, which means that it cannot be controlled, exactly as the serpent cannot be domesticated. They both elude us. Furthermore, the motions of the snake are marked out by anarchic animation and disorganised dynamism, which recall the wandering movements of imagination, equally irregular and lacking any identifiable predetermined destination, as they respond to the principles of divergent thinking. In addition, Keats relates his impression of writing almost at random, as if guided by a mysterious "Presider" (*Letters*, vol. 1, 142), and thus resorts to the Romantic myth of inspiration, which depends on the insights of unconscious imagination, as if arising from dictation by another. The idea of this 'other' acting during poetic creation and the related idea of the divine – i.e. unconscious – nature of the imagination lead to the identification of the serpent with the 'totally other' and its supernatural presentation. As a matter of fact, the symbol of the serpent and imagination seem so far to share their main characteristics. I will, therefore, proceed by considering the physical properties of snakes and see whether they have an equivalent in the Romantic – in particular, Keats's – model of the imagination.

When arguing for the unrelatedness of the serpent in *Aion*, Jung considers the fixity of its gaze as a further demonstration of its estrangement from man, even though it is more related to another aspect of snakes that is mentioned immediately before. In fact, Jung writes: "it *fascinates* [italics added]; its glance is staring, fixed, unrelated" (188). The fascinating power of the serpent has to be interpreted in its most literal sense, as it refers to the commonly held belief in the hypnotic quality of snakes' eyes. If Jung, however, does not give much importance to this feature of the serpent in his analysis of its symbolism, it is instead central in most of Keats's descriptions of snakes, partly due to his own sensibility and interests, as will be seen, and partly to those of his time. At the beginning of the 19th century, snakes' faculty of charming other animals, which is now dismissed as legendary fiction, was considered to be a scientific truth[82]. Among the causes of this mesmeric power, Romantic naturalists identified the mephitic breath exhaled by serpents, which Keats refers to in *Otho the Great*: "those two vipers, from whose jaws / A deadly breath went forth to taint and

---

81 See its association with heaven in "To J.H. Reynolds, Esq." (78–82), "Four seasons fill the measure of the year" (7) and *The Fall of Hyperion* (4).
82 See De Almeida 185–186.

blast / This guileless lady" (III ii 153–155). However, the passage lacks any specific mention of hypnotism, which both Keats and the scientists of his time ascribed mainly to another cause, that is, the serpent's stare.

It is, presumably, the absence of eyelids that originated the idea of the bewitching quality attributed to snakes' eyes by giving them a peculiarly fixed, glassy appearance[83], and, indeed, Keats constantly returns to this point. In "Song of Four Fairies", the element that relates Dusketha to the serpent are precisely her eyes (68: "Adder-eyed"), which are then defined as "bare unlidded eyes" (86). When Apollonius exerts his nefarious, hypnotic power over Lamia towards the end of the narration and paralyses her merely by staring at her, his eyes immediately acquire serpentine traits, such as an unnatural fixity (*Lamia* II 245–246: "The bald-head philosopher / Had fixed his eye, without a twinkle or stir"[84]) and the absence of lashes if not of lids (288–289: "Mark how, possessed, his lashless eyelids stretch / Around his demon eyes!"). Nevertheless, the most bewitching eyes in the poem are undoubtedly those of Lamia. Even though they are first described as human eyes on a snake's head due to her hybrid nature[85], they still have the serpent's ability to charm, as they are able to paralyse the fluttering Hermes, god of movement (Lamia I 66–67: "Hermes on his pinions lay, / Like a stooped falcon ere he takes his prey"), like snakes were thought to do with birds[86]. Her powers even seem to increase when she exerts them over Lycius. Immediately after showing no empathy whatsoever towards her suffering beloved, which has been identified as a typically serpent-like behaviour, she continues acting like a snake and charms him "if her eyes could brighter be, / With brighter eyes and slow amenity" (I, 292–293). A similar alluring quality belongs to the magical fire in Book 3 of *Endymion* and justifies its serpentine quality: the fire resembles "the eye of gordian snake" (494) precisely because it "bewitche[s]" (495). Lastly, in *Otho the Great*, Keats evokes the most famous of all serpents' glance, that is, the mythological cockatrice's: "O cockatrice, / I have you! Whither wander those fair eyes[87] / To entice the devil to your help, that he / May change you to a spider, so to crawl / Into some cranny to escape my wrath?" (V ii

---

83 See Hannah 159.
84 Keeping an eye contact with the victim is essential for the functioning of any hypnotic charm, which in serpents is facilitated precisely by the fact that lidless eyes cannot blink.
85 Her eyes are too "fair" (*Lamia* I 63) to belong to a serpent, and they show human sorrow by weeping (61–62: "what could such eyes do there / But weep, and weep, that they were born so fair"). Moreover, during her metamorphosis, her lashes are all seared (151), which points out that her eyes had lids and lashes.
86 "The fantastic phenomenon of birds that became paralyzed and fell or flew from branches into the waiting jaws of serpents became a focal point for all Romantic naturalists concerned with the subject" (De Almeida 186).
87 'Fair' is the same adjective used to describe Lamia's human eyes (*Lamia* I 63); Keats is referring here to Albert, a serpent-like man.

36–40). What is important to note is that Keats substitutes the killing faculty of the cockatrice with an enticing one and refers to animal swarming movement through the verb 'crawl'.

Apart from the eyes, the feature in the snake's appearance that usually draws most attention is its mouth, mostly due to the animal's ability to open it to an exceptional extent in order to swallow its entire prey. According to Jung, this is the reason why the serpent well represents the devouring aspect of the unconscious and its most dangerous side. However, Keats mentions the swallowing ability of the snake only once and in a very conventional context, where it is evoked simply as a menace: "the next after that shall see him necked, / Or swallowed by my hunger-starvèd asp" (*The Cap and Bells* 196–197). The other main element usually associated with the snake's mouth, that is, its poison, is marginalised as well, or rather it is evoked only to be denied. It is mentioned solely in *Hyperion*, where Iapetus's serpent "could not spit / Its poison in the eyes of conquering Jove" (II 47–48).

As a matter of fact, Keats seems to remove any reference to the devouring aspect of a serpent's predatory nature in order to focus on the hypnotic one, as is most evidently proven in *Lamia*, where the physical vampirism ascribed to the serpent-woman in the sources – as will be seen when dealing with them – is turned into an all psychological seduction. In fact, as soon as Lycius "look[s] back" (*Lamia* I 246) to Lamia and makes eye contact with her, he realises that he cannot ever turn his eyes from her[88], and he is so enthralled that he asserts: "Even as thou vanishes so I shall die" (I 260), which is precisely what is going to happen. This shift of focus from the mouth to the eyes is meaningful for at least two reasons. The former is that it is one of the two main elements of the serpent's presentation that favour its metapoetic interpretation. The serpent has been associated above with the imagination because of their corresponding properties, but without actually justifying why the symbolic significance of the serpent should work on a metaliterary level. By substituting the physical contact required in the act of swallowing or devouring with hypnotism, Keats depicts an animal that preys upon its victims from a certain distance[89]. This seduction from afar is exactly the same as poetry's. Concepts belonging to the practice of mesmerism were, in fact, used in the Romantic period to describe both the effect of poetry on its readers and, what is more important to the present analysis, the capacity of spontaneous inspiration to charm the poet's consciousness[90].

The link between mesmeric practice and creativity emerges most clearly

---

88 He utters: "Ah, Goddess, see / Whether my eyes can ever turn from thee!" (*Lamia* I 257–258) and in Book 2 he is still "bending to her open eyes" (46).
89 It is noteworthy that even the only venomous snake in Keats's poetry would not bite to inject poison but, rather, spit it (*Hyperion* II 47–48).
90 See DeLong 1–2.

when Keats[91] returns to the topos of poetic trance, as trance is precisely the psychophysiological condition that is produced by hypnosis. The most explicit case[92] is found in an early composition dedicated to his brother George and dated August 1816, where Keats describes the visions that occur in the mind "when a poet is in such a trance" ("To My Brother George" 25), as opposed to the lack of inspiration of the opening lines. This state of creative impasse is dominated by various fears, among which "That the bright glance from beauty's eyelids slanting / Would never make a lay of mine enchanting" (15-16). Both the hypnotic aspects of poetry are here suggested. Firstly, the composition is wished to possess a beguiling quality. The mesmerising power of poetry is made more explicit through the direct mention of the eyes a few months later in "Sleep and Poetry", where the "very archings of [Poesy's] eye-lids" is said to "charm / A thousand willing agents to obey" (239-238). Secondly, the enticing property is provided by the action of beauty's eyes presumably on the poet. This 'glancing', a verb which implies a very quick look, is quite different from the fixed 'staring' of snakes, and, indeed, "eyelids" ("To My Brother George" 15) are immediately mentioned, but the poem belongs to the very first phase of Keats's poetic career, when, as already seen, the symbol of the serpent did not seem to have become active yet. Nevertheless, the embryonic idea of the power of the eyes, which are "bright" (15), like those of Lamia (*Lamia* I 292-293), and the association of charming eyes with poetic inspiration are undoubtedly noteworthy. Moreover, the state of trance corresponds to the activation of the imagination, thanks to which the poet can behold "wonders strange" ("To My Brother George" 54). Seeing is presented here as the main activity of the entranced artist[93], which leads to the second significant aspect of Keats's focus on snakes' eyes, that is, the specific link between imagination and the eye itself, rather than its hypnotic power. 'Imagining' is, in fact, defined as a way of 'seeing' through the inward eyes, or, as Keats calls them in the letter about the spider, the "spiritual eye[s]" (*Letters*, vol. 1, 232). What imagination sparks within the poet are visions, so that the isotopy of sight is often evoked in relation to this poetic faculty[94].

---

91 Instances from other Romantic authors will be seen when dealing with Keats's sources.
92 At this point all the references made by Keats to the activation of imagination in an 'heightened state of consciousness' could be taken into account, since the phrase is a more generic definition which includes 'trance' as well.
93 "A sudden glow comes on them [those that love the bay], naught they *see* [italics added]/ In water, earth, or air, but poesy" (21-22); "when a poet is in such a trance, / In air he *sees* [italics added] white coursers paw and prance" (25-26); "The poet's *eye* [italics added] can reach those golden halls" (35); "much more would start into his *sight* [italics added]– / The revelries and mysteries of night. / And should I ever *see* [italics added] them, I will tell you / Such tales as needs must with amazement spell you" (63-64), where the spellbinding nature of poetry is mentioned as well.
94 Even if only the passages where the word 'imagination' occurs are considered – not those

The last physical characteristic of the serpent that Jung emphasises is its ability to shed its old skin and grow a new one, as if it were able to regenerate itself; thus Jung writes, "The snake, because it casts its skin, is a symbol of renewal" (Jung, *Symbols of Transformation* 269)[95]. Keats refers to the moulting in "Fancy", where he includes "the snake all winter-thin" that "Cast on sunny bank its skin" (57–58) among the pleasant sights from different seasons which fancy can bring together. This image undoubtedly stands for the revival of spring, like the "field-mouse" that "peep[s] / Meagre from its celled sleep" (55–56), while belonging to a poem that is explicitly metapoetic. As a result, the renewal of the snake's skin recalls fancy's ability to constantly provide new materials for poetic creation, which is mentioned also towards the end of "Ode to Psyche"[96], written only a few months later. As already mentioned, both these compositions present a fancy that partially overlaps imagination, but possesses some specific attributes as well. In any case, the most interesting mention of a serpent shedding its skin is found in Glaucus's invocation in Book 3 of *Endymion*: "O shell-borne Neptune, I am pierced and stung / With new-born life! What shall I do? Where go / When I have cast this serpent-skin of woe?" (238–240). The main underlying theme is again that of renewal, but it is interesting to note that the skin is clearly a metaphor for sorrow.

The association between serpent and pain occurs quite frequently in Keats's poetry and depends on features regarding the physical profile of snakes that Jung and Hannah do not take into account, as they do not seem to be part of the most recurrent intersubjective images of snakes. Thus, I will now focus on the most innovative and personal elements in Keats's presentation of serpents. It has already been pointed out that Keats never describes the movement of snakes precisely in terms of slithering and prefers to suggest the idea of unpredictable, anarchic motion that belong either to a sudden disappearance or to a slow creeping over the ground. Nevertheless, most of the verbs that are often used in

---

where its presence can be detected –, various instances of this isotopy are found: "Has she [the imagination] not *shown* [italics added] us all / From the clear space of ether to the small / Breath of new buds unfolding?" ("Sleep and Poetry" 167-169); "He could not bear it – shut his *eyes* [italics added] in vain. / Imagination gave a dizzier pain" (*Endymion* III 1008-1009, where the closing of the outer eyes corresponds to the opening of the inner ones); "It is a flaw / In happiness to *see* [italics added] beyond our bourn" ("To J.H. Reynolds, Esq." 82-83); "And in her wide imagination stood / Palm-shaded temples and high rival fanes" (*Hyperion* II 58-59, where there is no verb of sigh but an actual vision is described); "Since every man whose soul is not a clod / Hath *visions* [italics added]" (*The Fall of Hyperion* I 13-14); "even then you were mounted on the Wings of Imagination so high – that the Prototype must be here after – that delicious face you will *see* [italics added]" (*Letters*, vol. 1, 185); "My imagination is horribly vivid about her – I *see* [italics added] her" (*Letters*, vol. 2, 351).

95 See also Hannah 158.
96 "With all the gardener Fancy e'er could feign, / Who breeding flowers, will never breed the same" ("Ode to Psyche" 62-63).

conjunction with serpents suggest less a way of advancing in space than a contortion or convulsion of the snake's body[97]. In the already mentioned passage of Book 3 of *Endymion*, when the victims of Circes's spells form the image of the huge Python in the air, they are described by Glaucus "as by a whirlwind writhen" (529). 'Writhen' is the archaic past participle of 'to writhe', which, in the acceptation that became frequent at the beginning of the 19th century, stands for 'to contort the body, limbs, etc., as from agony, emotion, or stimulation; to twist *under* or *with* pain, distress, etc.; to wring, turn' (*OED*). The presence of a certain amount of suffering is implied in the meaning of the verb itself, which also suggests the idea of the same visually twisted forms[98] such as coiled serpents'.

In *The Fall of Hyperion* the branches of bare sable trees are compared with snakes precisely because of their twisted shape (446–447: "he sat beneath the sable trees, / Whose arms spread straggling in wild serpent forms"[99]), while in *Isabella* it is the neck of a distilling bottle that becomes a "cold serpent-pipe" (412) due to its sinuous form. In *Lamia*, the serpent-woman – at that moment endowed with a snake's body – is described by the narrator as "a gordian[100] shape of dazzling hue" (I 47), with reference to the legendary intricate knot, and she is invoked by Hermes as "beauteous wreath" (84). It is true that the wreath hints at a circular, and, therefore, simpler form[101], but it should be remembered that wreaths are made of twisted materials as well. Lamia herself defines her serpentine body as a "wreathed tomb" (I 38) where the adjective refers to her convoluted aspect rather than to the practice of laying garlands on graves. Just as Glaucus has to shed his "serpent-skin of woe" (*Endymion* III 240) in order to come back to life, so Lamia's condition in her "serpent prison-house" (*Lamia* I 203) resembles death. In both passages, the snake's skin or body appears to be a sort of constriction. Lamia gets rid of it not by literally moulting but by transforming herself, and it is during her metamorphosis that elements of the constellation of traits I am analysing are found again: "She writhed about, convulsed with scarlet pain" (I 154).

Proceeding with the parallel metapoetic discourse, the shapes of Keats's serpents present an intricacy that is reminiscent of the "most lovely labyrinths"

---

97 Both the verbs, however, imply some kind of movement, so that the serpent is never depicted as static, which is an important element as far as its elusive, dynamic animality and the consequent symbolism of the unconscious are concerned.
98 Keats's insistence on intricacy contrasts with Hannah's mention of the snake's simplicity of form (157–158).
99 "Straggling" indicates that they spread in an irregular way and, thus, is a further reference to chaotic animal movement.
100 The same adjective is referred to a serpent in *Endymion* III 494 ("gordian snake").
101 Lamia is presented as lying in circular coils through the neologism "cirque-couchant" (46) as well.

("Sleep and Poetry" 266) that imagination must go through during the creative act. In "On Receiving a Laurel Crown from Leigh Hunt" (18 April 1817), Keats returns to the same image and presents the missed outburst of inspiration in the following terms: "Minutes are flying swiftly, and as yet / Nothing unearthly has enticed my brain / Into a Delphic labyrinth" (1-3). These lines significantly present various elements I have so far insisted on. Inspiration coincides with the arising of contents from the unconscious imagination[102] – as if from another world – which affects the poet's conscious mind like an enticing power. If this is true, the labyrinth has a twofold meaning then: it stands for the wandering of the imagination because of its non-linear shape, but it may also convey the equally non-linear process of poetic composition, which goes from the initial outburst of inspiration to the final refined composition, whose difficulties Keats is well acquainted with, as will soon be argued.

Returning now to Lamia, not only does she writhe during her metamorphosis but she also undergoes convulsions. 'Convulse' is another verb that appears more than once in association with snakes and that means 'to affect with a succession of violent involuntary contractions of the muscles, so as to produce agitation of the limbs or whole body' (*OED*). 'Writhe' and 'convulse' are two related verbs, as they both apply to the movements of a body in pain, but the former stresses the contortion, whereas the latter focuses on the contraction. In Book 1 of *Hyperion*, as seen above, the serpent symbolises the "agony" that moves through the "bulk" (259) of the Titan, and the impression of overwhelming pain is conveyed through the fact that the snake has "head and neck convulsed / From over-strainèd might" (262-263). The spasms do not affect the serpent's whole body but are limited to head and neck. A focus on the same parts is found in Book 2, where Iapetus holds "in his grasp, / A serpent's plashy neck" (44-45). Here the contraction is caused by the Titan's grip rather than by involuntary stimuli in the snake, but the sense of constriction and suffocation is the same. Since the animal cannot spit its poison out against Jove, Iapetus holds it so tight that "its barbèd tongue / Squeezed from the gorge" (45-46). Although the representation of suffocated snakes clearly has its peak in *Hyperion*, its various elements are already present in the passage in Book 3 of *Endymion* about Python. Before going through the air like the mythological serpent "Antagonizing Boreas" (531), the "grieved bodies" (525) of the victims of Circe begin to "bloat / And puff from the tail's end to stifled throat" (525-526). Even though the painful suffocation is not directly related to the snake, it is interesting to note

---

102 In line 9 there is also the recurrent image of the dream to describe the product of poetic imagination: "Still time is fleeting, and no dream arises / Gorgeous as I would have it" ("On Receiving a Laurel Crown from Leigh Hunt" 9-10).

that, besides appearing only few lines above, it refers to the same animals that are going to be compared with Python.

The insistence on convulsions that concentrate in the neck implies a contraction of the throat and, thus, of the vocal canal, which leads to the second and most significant reason for a metapoetic interpretation of serpent symbolism. The throat is, in fact, the centre of the articulation of verbal expression, which, in its turn, constitutes the fundamental act of poetry. As already seen, according to Keats, "Poesy alone *can* [italics added] tell her dreams" (*The Fall of Hyperion* I 8) and, what is more, poets *must* tell their visions, or they will never be anything more than "fanatics" (1). The central problem of poetic verbalisation – for, as far as serpents are concerned, it is presented as a problem through the representation of an obstructed phonation – is related to imagination and, thus, confirms the signifying pattern that has been applied so far. What poets must tell are indeed their visions, i.e. the products of their imagination, but the communication of their imaginative insights is not effortless. As pointed out when dealing with Keats's conception of imagination, he enters into this issue especially in the verse letter to Reynolds, but hints at it whenever he refers to the necessity of restraining the imaginative faculty. If the language is articulated through the sequential laws of 'asymmetrical logic' and possesses the qualities of logical-formal thought[103], resorting to its means to give expression to imagination corresponds to an act of violence on the latter which, instead, belongs to 'symmetrical logic' and to the preverbal, even preconceptual dimension of the unconscious, as perfectly represented by the purely instinctual, non-cerebral nature of snakes. The restraint language imposes on imagination turns into the sense of constriction and pain which distinguishes the convulsed serpents I have mentioned, whose throats are so contracted that they cannot utter any sound. Ultimately, when turning to suffocated snakes, Keats seems to focus on the difficulty of the act of verbalisation rather than on searching for a compromise between the two faculties that makes poetry possible.

Sometimes, however, Keatsian serpents do succeed in emitting sound. In "Welcome joy and welcome sorrow" (October 1818), Keats includes "Serpents in red roses hissing" (15) among the coexisting contraries that the poem celebrates, while a hissing sound is present also in Book 2 of *Endymion*, where it renders the sibilant echo of a cave (233). Even if in absence of any direct reference to snakes, the hiss gives the place a serpentine quality by auditory suggestion, which is visually confirmed by its "winding passages", as "winding" is an adjective that indicates a twisting shape. Hissing is another ability of snakes that Jung does not take into account and is still related to the vocal canal. At this stage, I might now

---

103 Logical-formal thought and language have been associated since the ancient Greek notion of λόγος.

correct my previous assertion by saying that Keats shifts the focus from the devouring, poisonous mouth to the hypnotic eyes and the potentially sound-emitting throat. It is actually noteworthy that Keats's innovations compared with Jung's paradigm correspond to the elements that have the closest connection with poetic practice. This difference can be easily ascribed to the fact that Jung obviously has no metapoetic intention and poetic issues are not part of his worldview, unlike Keats's. Returning to the hiss emitted by serpents, however, the fact that they emit sound does not imply any achievement of poetic expression, as hissing belongs to the realm of animal noise rather than to the melodious songs of human poetry[104]. Even when snakes do not precisely hiss, as in *Isabella*, they "whine" (*Isabella* 190), that is, emit a high-pitched unpleasant sound that in this case stands for the deceit of Isabella's brothers towards Lorenzo. Ultimately, the dysphoric aspect of noise[105] is one more element that associates the serpent with the difficulty – not the success – of verbalisation.

Furthermore, Keats puns on the opposition between noise and music in the term "hissing" itself ("Welcome joy and welcome sorrow" 15), which appears as if composed of 'hiss' and 'sing'. The word gives lexical form to the bipolar relationship between the inarticulate and the articulate, which is only potential, as 'sing' is contained in the present participle of 'hiss'. This pattern is reproduced in the phonosymbolic structure of the whole of line 15, which concentrates voiceless sounds – which are nearer to dysphoric noise – at the beginning and at the end ("S̲e̲rp̲en̲t̲s̲" and "h̲i̲s̲s̲ing") whereas voiced one – which are nearer to euphoric human voice – in the middle ("i̲n̲ r̲ed r̲oses"). Whether musicality is actually latent in noise is an unresolved question, but it is noteworthy that the serpent, while evoking the tension between these two opposites, and thus con-

---

104 Besides the topical nature of the comparison between poetry and song, Keats refers to poetry in musical terms throughout his whole production: "Sweet are the pleasures that to verse belong, / And doubly sweet a brotherhood in *song* [italics added]" ("To George Felton Mathew" 1–2); "That I should never hear Apollo's *song* [italics added]" ("To My Brother George" 9); "that you first taught me all the sweets of *song* [italics added]" ("To Charles Cowden Clarke" 53); "What first inspired a bard of old to *sing* [italics added]" ("I stood tip-toe upon a little hill" 163); "So while the poet stood in this sweet spot, / Some fainter gleamings o'er his fancy shot, / Nor was it long ere he had told the tale / Of young Narcissus, and sad Echo's bale / Where had he been, from whose warm head out-flew / The sweetest of all *songs* [italics added]" (177–182); "that I may dare, in wayfaring, / To stammer where old Chaucer used to *sing* [italics added]" (*Endymion* I 133–134); "that the free, / The buoyant life of *song* [italics added] can floating be / Above their heads and follow them untired" (IV 351–353); "my *song* [italics added] should die away" ("Ode to May" 12); "Oh, leave them, Muse! Oh, leave them to their woes; / For thou art weak to sing such tumults dire" (*Hyperion* III 3–4); "I see, and *sing* [italics added], by my own eyes inspired" ("Ode to Psyche" 43: this line can be considered a condensation of Keats's poetics).
105 At the beginning of Book 2 of *Lamia*, "distrust and hate" are said to "make the soft voice hiss" (10), thus opposing euphoric human musicality with dysphoric hissing.

firming once more its nature of 'living symbol', remains more directly associated with the realm of inarticulate sounds. The words that belong semantically to the snake, i.e. "Serpents" and "hissing", contain various voiceless phonemes, whereas the voiced ones help to define the roses, which the poem identifies as their opposite, though in a relation of coexistence[106], as exemplified by the vocal elements that have been analysed.

Nevertheless, Keats's poetry includes the surprising case of a serpent that seems to fulfil its singing potential, too. In fact, not only does Lamia hypnotise Lycius with her bright eyes, but she also entices him through her "song of love, too sweet for earthly lyres" (*Lamia* I 298). If Keats usually compares poetic expression with singing, the charming power of Lamia's song further equates it with poetry, which, as already noted, according to Keats, possesses a certain beguiling quality. Moreover, a very similar phrase occurs in "I stood tip-toe upon a little hill" (Dec. 1816) defining the imaginative material of poetic composition: "Shapes from the invisible world, unearthly singing / From out the middle air" (186-187). According to the interpretations that I have applied so far, on a metapoetic level, the unearthliness of Lamia's song indicates that it draws directly from the unconscious realm of imagination and is able to do so because it works precisely like a spell. Lamia's musical voice, which irresistibly binds Lycius to her, is indeed an important part of her magical practices[107]. In order to better understand the significance of this element, it should be remembered that a reference to charms is again present in the fundamental opening lines of *The Fall of Hyperion*. Here Keats does not seem to consider the verbalisation of the poet's visions as a problem, since he can convey them through "the fine spell of words" (I 9). Spells are verbal components of magic, which is a system of beliefs and behaviours whose aim is to impose the human will on nature by exploiting the sympathetic relations and connections that make the whole universe cohere together. In other words, magic works through sympathy[108] – indeed, Lamia seduces Lycius by inducing an extreme empathy in him, so that he becomes completely dependent on her emotionally[109]. Sympathy is a central faculty in the

---

106 The composition celebrates the compresence of opposites as said in the firs lines: "Welcome joy and welcome sorrow [...] I do love you both together" (1, 4).
107 These practices include her ability to cover great distances in a very short amount of time (*Lamia* I 344-346: "The way was short, for Lamia's eagerness / Made, by a spell, the triple league decrease / To a few paces") and to build an enchanted palace (see I 378-393 and II 115-124, 150-155).
108 For an introduction on sympathy which pays particular attention to its relation to magic, see Lobis 6-35. Lobis also quotes a passage by Plotinus where the philosopher argues that magic spells work by sympathy (7), which is an interesting finding, even if Keats presumably never read it.
109 Lycius asserts: "So sweetly to these ravished ears of mine / Came thy sweet greeting, that if thou shouldst fade / Thy memory will waste me to a shade" (*Lamia* I 268-270). He is

Romantic conception of the world and of creativity as well[110] and, what is more, it is involved in the process through which the poet communicates his insight to the reader. Being based on the sympathetic ability of the writer to enter into contact with the public's feelings, the passage from vision to words, according to Romantic ideals, should be as spontaneous and effortless as the outburst of inspiration within the poet. As a result, through the "delicious" (*Lamia* I 249) singing of Lamia, Keats seems to hint at a different resolution of the problem of poetic expression, which corresponds more closely to Romantic principles.

What has still to be ascertained is whether this alternative conception of verbalisation, which conflicts with the one that has been associated so far with the serpent, is represented equally well by this symbol. Actually, the fact that it works through sympathy suggests a negative answer, since the cold-blooded, heedless, unrelated snakes lack any 'empathy', to refer here to the contemporary term corresponding to the Romantic preferred choice, 'sympathy'. The emergence of her predatory, serpentine nature prevents Lamia from behaving empathically towards her beloved Lycius (*Lamia* I 290-295), but at the same time she is able to express herself in a way that, as just seen, can be ascribed to the working of sympathy. This seeming contradiction is explained by the fact that Lamia is not entirely a snake but rather a snake-woman, so that her nature is always twofold. Her charming voice has actually been connoted as human since the very first description of her hybrid aspect: "Her throat was serpent, but the words she spake / Came, as through bubbling honey, for love's sake" (I 64-65). The adversative conjunction stresses the incompatibility between snakes and the emission of melodious sounds. A singing serpent inevitably appears as something unnatural. If Lamia's nature is always twofold, however, even her voice does not belong entirely to the euphoric domain of musicality, but shows traces of dysphoric noise. Hermes calls her "smooth-lipped serpent, surely high inspired" (I 83), so resorting to the lexicon of poetical inspiration, yet when she asks him to turn her into a woman, she speaks "swift-lisping" (I 116), which is a neologism to indicate a rapid way of speaking marked by a defective pronunciation of the 's'. This emphasis on sibilants suggests the hiss of snakes, while the speech impediment a difficulty of emission and an unmelodious sound that is nearer to noise than to singing, as conveyed too by the fact that the sibilants in "swift-lisping" are voiceless.

The coexistence of axiologically opposite traits, such as those of music and noise, is not limited to the hybrid nature of the snake-woman, but, as a matter of

---

subjected to an extreme form of empathy with Lamia, as he is bound to physically experience what she goes through. The capacity of placing oneself in another's position, which constitutes one of the definitions of empathy, is here taken literally.

110 Sympathy belongs to Keats's view of creativity as well, since, as already seen, he partly draws on it to develop his idea of negative capability.

fact, belongs to the symbol of the serpent as well. When discussing about the definition of the snake as 'living symbol' in Keats's poetry, the importance of ambivalence has been stressed, since it provides the symbol with its tensional energy. I will now insist on this fundamental point once more, as it is a central element of the traditional, intersubjective representation of serpents too. Jung asserts that the serpent is "both toxic and prophylactic, equally a symbol of the good and bad daemon" (Jung, *Symbols of Transformation* 374), as it stands both for "the lowest (the devil) and the highest (son of God[)]" (Jung, *Aion* 188). Even its capability of symbolising the unconscious is determined by its duplicity, and that of the human attitude towards it:

> its cold blood and inferior brain-organization do not suggest any noticeable degree of conscious development, while its unrelatedness to man makes it an alien creature that arouses his fear and yet fascinates him. Hence it is an excellent symbol for the two aspects of the unconscious: its cold and ruthless instinctuality, and its Sophia quality or natural wisdom (Jung, *Alchemical Studies* 333).

Keats's snakes do not have a fixed axiological value either. Even though some of them seem to be exclusively negative, the bivalent ones are more numerous and more interesting. It has been stated that, in order to be considered a 'living symbol', the serpent needs to possess unresolved opposite connotations, which is true when the representation of snakes in Keats's whole production is considered, but that consideration should remain valid as far as individual serpents are concerned too. In fact, it is not by chance that the less ambiguous snakes on an axiological level are found in more conventional contexts and do not usually present the Keatsian innovative features that have been pointed out[111]. Exclusively negative snakes function as menaces[112], or insults[113], or are used to proverbially indicate treacherous people[114]. Their mention is topical and con-

---

111 The Pedrinis point out that "Keats's rather heavy reliance on classical mythology may explain in part the conventionality of many of the serpent images in his poetry" (50) and they quote two passages from *Otho the Great* (III ii 152–155 and V ii 36–40). If it is true that the serpents in the tragedy are depicted in a rather conventional way, it is not correct to extend this opinion to Keats's general serpent imagery, which, as already seen, presents some innovative elements and is more inspired by Milton and Coleridge than by classical sources.
112 "And the next after that shall see him necked, / Or swallowed by my hunger-starvèd asp – / And mention ('tis as well) the torture of the wasp" (*The Caps and the Bells* 196-198).
113 "Yet why do I delay to spread abroad / The names of those two vipers, from whose jaws / A deadly breath went forth to taint and blast / This guileless lady?" (*Otho the Great* III ii 152–155); "A snake, / A scorpion, sprawling on the first gold step, / Conducting to the throne high canopied" (IV i 14–16); "O cockatrice, / I have you! Whither wander those fair eyes / To entice the devil to your help, that he / May change you to a spider, so to crawl / Into some cranny to escape my wrath?" (V ii 36–40).
114 "Lorenzo, courteously as he was wont, / Bowed a fair greeting to these serpents' whine" (*Isabella* 189–190).

ventional, and lacks the ambivalence that is necessary for the activation of a 'living symbol' as well as the features that would lead to a metapoetic interpretation[115]. They work more as metaphors, since they can be decoded easily and univocally. In *Isabella*, for instance, the serpents stand for the deceitful brothers (190), whereas the vipers in *Otho the Great* stand for slanderers (III ii 153). This is why I will not focus on them in my analysis. Moreover, the ambivalence of snake symbolism has been recalled here, even though it is not a physical characteristic, because it is a further corresponding element linking the serpent with the imagination. In fact, the chapter about Keats's conception of creativity has shown that imagination is not always exalted by Keats, as would be expected of a Romantic poet; it is sometimes presented through its risky and even negative aspects too[116].

In conclusion, it is important to restate that the correspondences detected here between physical features of the serpent and the properties of imagination do not mean that the serpent *stands for* the imagination. That would be so if the snake worked as a metaphor in Keats's works, but I have already argued in favour of interpreting it as a 'living symbol'. As a result, 'imagination' is not the unique referent of the serpent, nor does the latter figuratively substitute the former. Their relationship does not work through a mimetic principle, since their analogies are arbitrary and depend on a cultural model of imagination. Furthermore, the serpent is less related to the imagination in its entirety than to the specific issue of the emergence of imaginative insights[117] and their verbalisation, so that the two terms cannot be simply equated. Ultimately, the serpent as 'living symbol' conveys something that Keats is experiencing during poetic creation and arises from the problem of turning his visions into words. The contrast between the symmetrical functioning of imagination and the asymmetrical laws of language provides the tension which stands at the origin of every living

---

115 There are also serpents that work as a 'living symbol' without any metapoetic interpretation, such as the aspic in the following lines of "Welcome joy and welcome sorrow": "Cleopatra regal-dressed / With the aspic at her breast" (16–17). A correspondence can be found between these lines and the previous one (15: "Serpents in red roses hissing"), even though the latter presents a metapoetic meaning that has been already analysed. In lines 15–16 the snake is not hidden in roses but both in Cleopatra's dress and in her breast. The hiding place has doubled and the two outcomes are in opposition. They both belong to the isotopy of regality that dominates the figure of Cleopatra and is confirmed by the parallel with the red roses, which are regal flowers of a regal colour. However, the royal garment, together with the emblem of the red rose, symbolise a positive, masculine power, whereas the rosy breast stands for feminine excellence and thus a negative, womanly power. The two coexist in the same bipolar symbol.
116 See, in particular, the quoted passages of "To J.H. Reynolds" (78–85), "On Visiting the Tomb of Burns" (8–12) and *Letters*, vol. 1, 293.
117 The emergence of the insight to consciousness is acknowledged by cognitive psychology as a stage of the creative process (see Sawyer 67–68).

symbol, but, just as this fundamental metapoetic paradigm remains constant, the specific aspects of poetic verbalisation that take shape through the symbol, as well as the attitude towards it, continue to change throughout Keats's works.

3.2 Sources

If it is true that the serpent is a culturally determined symbol, it is only natural that Keats should find it in the products of culture he is most familiar with, that is, in literary tradition, and, thanks to the features that have been analysed in the previous chapter, this image strikes him with its ability to convey what he feels the urge to express about his own creative process. Since any attempt to take into account all the occurrences of snakes in literary works that Keats read would take too long and be impracticable, I will here focus solely on the specific sources of Keats's snakes. Some texts function chiefly as collections of myths and stories that provide Keats, first of all, with narrative plots, but sometimes with interesting aspects of characterisation too. For instance, the story of the mythical Python, which Keats mentions directly in *Endymion* (III 530–531) and implicitly in *Lamia* (II 78–80), is drawn from Lempriére's *Classical Dictionary* (1788) and from Sandys's translation of Ovid's *Metamorphoses* (1632), Keats's two main sources for classical mythology[118]. There is a sharp difference, though; Lempriére merely supplies a narration of Python's life and death[119], whereas the lines from Sandys also associate the serpent's body with movement, whose importance in Keats's presentations of snakes has been stressed above: "Python / A Serpent, whom the new-borne People dread; / Whose bulk did like a moving

---

118   Lempriére was present in Keats's library as recorded in the catalogue by Ownings (39), and Charles Cowden Clarke remembers Keats reading it with such zeal that "he appeared to *learn*" (124) it. He considers it among "his constantly recurrent sources of attraction" as well as "the store whence he acquired his intimacy with the Greek mythology" (*ibidem*) during the last eighteen months he attended school. By contrast, Sandys is not mentioned in Ownings' catalogue, but it is acknowledged as one of Keats's main sources as far as classical myths are concerned by critics such as Bush (85) and Colvin (*Keats: Narrative poems* 75–76). What is true is that Keats is influenced by Sandys on a formal – and in particular metrical – level too, as Bate points out dealing with Keats's use of run-on first lines in *Lamia* (156–157).

119   "A celebrated serpent sprung from the mud and stagnant waters which remained on the surface of the earth after the deluge of Deucalion. Some, however, suppose that it was produced from the earth by Juno, and sent by the goddess to persecute Latona, who was then pregnant by Jupiter. Latona escaped his fury by means of her lover, who changed her into a quail during the remaining months of her pregnancy and afterwards restored her to her original shape in the island of Delos, where she gave birth to Apollo and Diana. Apollo, as soon as he was born, attacked the monster and killed him with his arrows, and in commemoration of the victory which he had obtained, he instituted the celebrated Pythian games" (Lempriére 540).

Mountaine showe" (I 438-440). In Sandys, Keats finds the link between Alecto and serpents as well (X 313-314: "Alecto, with swolne snakes, and Stygian fire / That furie rais'd"), which he resorts to in Book 2 of *Endymion* (874-875)[120]. Moreover, the adjective 'swollen' is reminiscent of the bloating of Circe's victims before she takes on the form of Python in Book 3 (525). Their "stifled throat[s]" (526) are among the first hints at suffocation to be loosely linked with snakes at this stage, when smothering is suggested by swelling rather than by contraction.

As far as *Lamia* is concerned, the story comes from a passage of Burton's *Anatomy of Melancholy*[121], another of Keats's main sources[122], which he himself added to the 1820 edition of *Lamia, Isabella, The Eve of St. Agnes and Other Poems*. Even if the text presents various interesting points when compared with Keats's poem[123], I will focus here on how the serpent is present, or, rather, on its absence. The passage is as follows:

> *Philostratus* in his fourth book *de vita Apollonii*, hath a memorable instance in this kinde, which I may not omit, of one *Mennipus Lycius*, a young man twenty-five yeares of age, that going betwixt *Cenchreas* and *Corinth*, met such a phantasme in the habit of a faire gentlewoman, which taking him by the hand carried him home to her house in the suburbs of *Corinth*, and told him she was a *Phoenician* by birth, and if hee would tarry with her, *he would heare her sing and play, and drinke such wines as never any dranke, and no man should molest him; but she, being faire and lovely, would live and dye with him that was faire and lovely to behold*. The young man a Philosopher, otherwise staid and discreet, able to moderate his passions, though not his love, tarried with her awhile to his great content, and at last married her, to whose wedding amongst other guests, came *Apollonius*, who, by some probable conjectures, found her out to be a serpent, *a Lamia*, and that all her furniture was like *Tantalus* gold described by *Homer*, no sub-

---

120 The association necessarily derives from Sandys, as the original does not present the proper name of the Fury but a more generic "una soror" (X 314).
121 The other occurrences of snakes in Burton are not exceedingly significant: they are mentioned among other animals as similes for moral characteristics (vol. 1, 52) or outcomes of metamorphoses (vol. 1, 197); they are used in a derogatory way (vol. 3, 19 and 208) or to indicate Eden's serpent (vol. 3, 274); they are present in tales of melancholic people who believe they have swallowed snakes or frogs (vol. 1, 412 and vol. 2, 112). Apart from Lamia's story, the only passage that seems to have directly inspired Keats refers to the adder's ability to stop its ears (vol. 1, 316), which returns as the only mention of a serpent in Keats's letters (*Letters*, vol. 2, 177).
122 Burton is recorded in the catalogue of Keats's books (17) and his influence on Keats's poetry has been pointed out by many critics, such as Sinson in *John Keats and the Anatomy of Melancholy* and Ward in "Keats and Burton: A Reappraisal".
123 Keats follows his source rather faithfully, but he departs from it in some significant points: the introduction of Hermes and the nymph as a frame, the personal tie between Lycius and Apollonius, Lycius's rebellion against his instructor and his eventual death. Chambers, while dealing with *Lamia*'s important debt to Burton, points out that the opening episode is not directly inspired by this source (589), while Murry insists on Keats's departure from his source as far as Lycius's relationship with Apollonius and his death are concerned (157). Lycius's death is considered as the major departure from Burton by Stewart, too (35).

stance, but meere illusions. When she saw her selfe descried, she wept, and desired *Apollonius* to be silent, but he would not be moved, and thereupon, she, Plate, House, and all that was in it, vanished in an instant: *many thousands took notice of this fact, for it was done in the midst of Greece* (Burton, vol. 3, 45–46).

Lamia appears as a fair woman at the beginning and is revealed to be a serpent only at the end without ever being described. Apart from her supernatural nature[124] and her final disappearance, which are features shared by Keats's serpent as well, it is noteworthy that Burton does not mention the creature's intention of devouring the young man. The story of Menippus Lycius does not come from Burton's imagination, but is taken from the *Life of Apollonius of Tyana*, written by Lucius Flavius Philostratus between the second and third century A.D. Even though Keats did not have access to this text, it is interesting to note that the story told here belongs to the genre of ancient tales of vampirism[125], whereas Burton does not refer to the female creature as a vampire. However, the choice of eliminating physical vampirism in favour of seduction from afar, whose relevance has already been pointed out, is as much Keats's as Burton's. Keats, in fact, could have been made aware of the devouring habits of the *lamiae* through Lemprière's *Classical Dictionary*. The entry for "Lamiae" is as follows:

> Certain monsters of Africa, who had the face and breast of a woman, and the rest of their body like that of a serpent. They allured strangers to come to them, that they might devour them; and though they were not endowed with the faculty of speech, yet their hissings were pleasing and agreeable. Some believed them to be witches, or rather evil spirits, who, under the form of a beautiful woman, enticed young children and devoured them (Lemprière 317).

Though both versions of the story insist on the enticing power as well as the devouring one of the *lamiae*, Keats retains only the former and even enriches it through the element of hypnotic eyes. In fact, Lemprière's *lamiae*, whose hybrid aspect is a probable source for Lamia[126], do not allure men through their eyes, but, apparently, through their hissings, which are unnaturally pleasant. The idea of charming, euphoric sound is undoubtedly inspiring for Keats, who, however,

---

124 The supernatural identity of the serpent-woman is emphasised by the fact that the story is included in the paragraph that shows how "the spirits of the aire, and divells of hell themselves [...] are as much inamored and dote (if I may use that word) as any other creatures whatsoever" (Burton, vol. 3, 45). The effects of love on humans are dealt with in the following chapter, "How Love tyrannizeth over Men" (48).

125 "Apollonius insisted relentlessly, until it [the phantom] confessed it was a vampire, fattening Menippus with pleasures in order to feed on his body, since it was its custom to *devour* [italics added] beautiful young bodies because their blood was fresh" (Philostratus 377).

126 In fact, Burton presents the woman and the serpent as two different stages that do not intersect.

goes further and endows Lamia with a faculty of speech that is denied to her mythical counterparts. In addition, both Burton and Lemprière seem to use 'Lamia' as a common noun, whereas Keats turns it into a name without altogether removing the traditional meaning[127]. The idea may be suggested to him by another myth about a woman called Lamia, which immediately follows the quoted passage in Lemprière:

> According to some, the fable of the Lamiae is derived from the amours of Jupiter with a certain beautiful woman called Lamia, whom the jealousy of Juno rendered deformed, and whose children she destroyed; upon which Lamia became insane, and so desperate that she ate up all the children that came in her way (Lemprière 317).

Even though this tale seems to share nothing with the poem, its interest lies in the fact that Lamia is a woman and, what is more, a good natured one, who turns evil because of the sufferings inflicted on her. To sum up, when he was about to start composing *Lamia*, three different figures must have occurred to Keats's mind under the same name – a serpent-like creature able to create illusions, a hybrid monster who devours men, and an innocent woman driven mad by grief.

These sources mainly provide Keats with the story and the characters for *Lamia* but do not account for the description of the serpent in the poem (I 45–65), which is probably inspired by a passage in *Paradise Lost*[128]:

> Circular base of rising folds, that tow'r'd
> Fold above fold a surging Maze; his Head
> Crested aloft, and Carbuncle his Eyes;
> With burnisht Neck of verdant Gold, erect
> Amidst his circling Spires, that on the grass
> Floated redundant [...] (IX 498–503)

In these lines that Keats marked in his own copy of the poem[129], Milton gives prominence to the spires of Eden's serpent, in particular, both to their circular shape and their labyrinthine intricacy, which Keats renders with "cirque-couchant" (*Lamia* I 46) and "gordian shape" (47), respectively. The latter aspect has been shown to recur in Keats's depiction of snakes, and Milton's metaphor of the maze reinforces the comparison that has been drawn between the twisted shape of the serpent and the "labyrinths" of imagination ("Sleep and Poetry" 266). It may work as a sort of middle term that makes explicit the relation between the two elements. In addition, although the metaphor of the labyrinth is not directly applied to the shape of serpents by Keats, it is probably hidden in *Lamia*'s lines: "Lycius from death awoke into amaze, / To see her still, and singing so sweet lays"

---

127 See Slote 142.
128 The link between the two passages is pointed out by Allott in a note on page 618 of her edition of Keats's poems.
129 The annotated copy of Milton is mentioned in Owings' catalogue (45).

(*Lamia* I 322-323), where "into amaze" can also be read as "into a maze"[130] in order to indicate the condition of enthrallment Lamia induces in Lycius through her singing. A parallel can be found precisely in Milton who creates a pun out of Eve's amazement[131] and the snake's "Maze" (*Paradise Lost* IX 499). The latter is, indeed, the agent of her bewilderment, as it stands both for his twisted body and the subtlety of his argument[132]. The intricate form of Eden's snake is further insisted on in the following lines: "of his tortuous Train / Curl'd many a wanton wreath in sight of Eve, / To lure her Eye" (*Paradise Lost* IX 516-518). 'Wreath' is exactly the same word used by Hermes to define Lamia in line 84, and the serpent relies on his aspect to seduce Eve just as Lamia's "dazzling" (*Lamia* I 47) appearance induces Hermes to stop and listen to her request. As far as the link between the serpent and imagination is concerned, Keats may have been inspired too by Milton's phrase "with Serpent error wand'ring" (*Paradise Lost* VII 302), where the course of a river is conveyed by using the term that Keats and the Romantics apply to the activity of the imaginative faculty[133].

In addition, Keats takes from Milton's snake other physical features[134], such as its radiant colours and its "Crested" (*Paradise Lost* IX 500) head. As far as the former are concerned, Eden's serpent has a "burnisht Neck of verdant Gold" (501), later described as "sleek enamell'd" (525), and "Carbuncle [...] Eyes" (500) that glow like coal. If it is true that Lamia is equally shiny and lustrous (*Lamia* I 51-53: "full of silver moons, that, as she breathed, / Dissolved, or brighter shone, or interwreathed / Their lustres with the gloomier tapestries"), her colours are even more luxuriant, as she is "Vermillion-spotted, golden, green and blue" (I 48) and her skin has such multifarious patterns that it is compared to that of various animals. Lamia is, in fact, "Striped like a zebra, freckled like a pard, / Eyed like a peacock, and all crimson barred" (I 49-50). Thus, even if Lamia's human traits are overlooked, Keats still ascribes to her a hybrid aspect that does not derive from his source and that belongs to Dusketha as well in "Song of Four Fairies"[135]. Like Eden's snake (*Paradise Lost* IX 525: "his turret Crest"), Lamia also has a "crest" and upon it she wears a "wannish fire / Sprinkled with stars, like Ariadne's tiar" (*Lamia* I 57-58), which is another element that is inspired by Milton, in particular by a line Keats marks in his copy

---

130 See O'Neill 134.
131 She is "Not unamaz'd" (*Paradise Lost* IX 552) and then "more amaz'd" (614).
132 For the relation between the mazy shape of Eden's serpent, Eve's amazement and the labyrinths of verbal seduction, see Swaim 132-140.
133 See what has been pointed out about the verb 'wander' in the paragraph about imagination.
134 For a survey of Keats's debts to Milton's description of Eden's snake, see Gordon 435-437.
135 Dusketha is said to be "freckle-winged and lizard-sided" ("Song of Four Fairies" 74), which suggests that, although she has the eyes of an adder, she is not a snake, or rather there is no reason to believe so.

of *Paradise Lost:* "the blasted Stars lookt wan" (X 412). Since the line belongs to the description of Sin and Death's journey from Hell to Earth, referring to it may be a further hint at the demonic side of Lamia's nature, who has just been compared to the "demon's mistress, or the demon's self" (*Lamia* I 56). 'Wan' or 'wannish' both convey the idea of a liminality regarding light, since they refer to a fire that shines in a very dim way but has not been extinguished yet. A further hint at a similar liminality between light and darkness is found in the name of Dusketha, as 'dusk' indicates the transition from day to night. It is noteworthy that, in both cases, Keats's reference to in-between light conditions corresponds to the ontological liminality, i.e. hybridism, of the characters that are being described. Furthermore, the image of a serpent with a pointed crest may have been suggested too by the illustration of Hermione in Sandys's *Ovid*, where she appears as half a crowned woman and half a snake. Her hybrid aspect may have inspired Keats, even though he does not neatly distinguish between a human part and a serpentine one in Lamia, but rather intermixes elements of the two[136].

Ultimately, both Lamia and Eden's snake are distinguished by beguiling beauty: if Lamia is a "beauteous wreath" (*Lamia* I 84), Milton's serpent possesses a "pleasing [...] shape / And lovely" (*Paradise Lost* IX 503–504), lovelier than any other serpent, including Cadmus and Hermione (506). It is the second time Hermione – also known as Harmonia – is mentioned, and, indeed, her and Cadmus's myth is important to Keats for two reason. Firstly, it is Keats's most significant source for entirely good serpents[137], whereas all other texts seem to prefer the evil connotations of snakes[138]. Keats's acquaintance with both positive and negative serpents is important, since it helps to provide the fundamental axiological ambiguity of the symbol. Secondly, the description of their metamorphosis in Sandys is an example of the transformation of mortals into serpents that is reversed in *Lamia*. Cadmus, the founder of Thebes, spends his old age afflicted with misfortune as a result of his having killed the water-dragon that guarded the Ismenian spring. If the life of the serpent was so sacred to the Gods, Cadmus remarks, he wishes he were one as well, and the Gods immediately fulfil his desire. Although his metamorphosis shows no close parallel to that of Lamia, it is interesting to note that both texts define tears[139] and voice as specifically

---

136 See the plate in Book 4: http://ovid.lib.virginia.edu/sandys/bk4start.htm.
137 "These gentle Dragons, knowing what they were, / Doe hurt to no man, nor mans presence feare" (*Ovid's Metamorphosis* IV 605–606).
138 The most extreme case is Milton's retelling of the biblical account of the Fall, where the serpent is responsible for Eve's seduction and man's original sin. It is, however, noteworthy that Milton's snake is not intrinsically evil but made so by Satan. Immediately after the creation, he is defined as "Not noxious" (*Paradise Lost* VII 498) and as innocent as all other God's creatures.
139 Cadmus sheds "teares [...] that yet were humane" (*Ovid's Metamorphosis* IV 584), like

human features. In fact, as soon as Cadmus turns into a snake, he is "of humane speech bereft" (*Ovid's Metamorphosis* IV 590) and "hist, when he his sorrowes sought to vent; / The only language now which Nature lent" (591–592). The human ability to articulate one's own feelings through language is openly contrasted with the serpent's hiss belonging to the realm of inarticulate noise. What is more, it is precisely the possibility of expression, which is the problem Keats confronts on a poetic level, to be denied to Cadmus. Lastly, at the end of the metamorphosis the serpents present some of the characteristics that have already been seen to be typical of Keatsian snakes: they are bright, crested (IV 603: "glittering combs"), and, above all, they creep with intertwined bodies (603: "crept, together chayn'd").

As Lamia is a serpent that, due to her hybrid nature, is exceptionally endowed with the faculty of speech, so Keats finds an unusually speaking snake in his sources too. It is again the case of Milton's serpent that seduces Eve not only through his lovely appearance but also through his words. As a matter of fact, Eve seems to be more impressed by the fact that the snake can speak than by what he says to her. She marvels at his speech and wonders:

> What may this mean? Language of Man pronounc't
> By Tongue of Brute, and human sense exprest?
> The first at least of these I thought deni'd
> To Beasts, whom God in their Creation-Day
> Created mute to all articulate sound;
> The latter I demur, for in their looks
> Much reason, and in their actions oft appears.
> Thee, Serpent, subtlest beast of all the field
> I knew, but not with human voice endu'd. (*Paradise Lost* IX 553–561)

A speaking serpent appears to Eve as something supremely unnatural, an outright "miracle" (562), which violates natural laws and depends on Satan's mischief. The insistence on the serpent's incompatibility with verbal communication is present in both Sandys and Milton, which means that it is rather likely to have drawn Keats's attention. Nevertheless, Milton's speaking serpent does not possess the same musical voice as Lamia, nor does he sing. In a few words, the vocal attributes that are most directly linked with poetic expression are not found in Keats's sources.

Paradise Lost has proven to be Keats's most important source so far[140], and,

---

Lamia's fair human eyes cannot but "weep" (*Lamia* I 62) that they were born on a serpent's head.

140 In his own copy of *Paradise Lost*, Keats marked different passages regarding serpents, not only all the lines describing Satan in the guise of the snake in Book 9 (158–161, 179–191, 499–510, 512, 516–517, 525–526, 631–643, 664–678, 1068), but also lines 447–449 in Book 4, lines 483–483 and 496–497 in Book 7, lines 524–528, 559–560 and 580–581 in Book 10. Lau

indeed, there is still one more serpent's feature that is inspired by Milton, that is, its connection with suffocation. Eden's snake was not created evil by God but became so due to Satan's wicked intervention. The account of the devil entering the serpent is as follows:

> Like a black mist low creeping, he held on
> His midnight search, where soonest he might find
> The Serpent: him fast sleeping soon he found
> In Labyrinth of many a round self-roll'd,
> His head the midst, well stor'd with subtle wiles;
> Not yet in horrid Shade or dismal Den,
> Nor nocent yet, but on the grassy Herb
> Fearless, unfear'd, he slept: in at his Mouth
> The Devil enter'd, and his brutal sense,
> In heart or head, possessing soon inspir'd
> With act intelligential; but his sleep
> Disturb'd not, waiting close th'approach of Morn. (IX 180-191)

Not only does Keats mark this passage in his copy of Milton, but he also writes an illuminating comment next to it: "Satan having entered the Serpent, and inform'd his brutal sense – might seem sufficient – but Milton goes on 'but his sleep disturb'd not' &c. Whose spirit does not ache at the smothering and confinement – the unwilling stillness – the 'waiting close'? Whose head is not dizzy at the prosiable speculations of Satan in this serpent prison – no passage of poetry ever can give a greater pain of suffocation"[141]. Besides the further use of the labyrinth as metaphor for the snake's coiled body (183), the passage from Milton is remarkable because of its relation with *Hyperion* I 259-263. Even though Milton's lines are usually thought to have inspired Keats's one[142], the actual contact between the two texts is rather loose. If Milton describes Satan entering the snake, Keats depicts agony penetrating like a serpent in Hyperion's body. The container and the contained are thus reversed. However, it is Keats's comment that allows to understand the proper link between the two passages by highlighting the central theme of suffocation.

According to Keats, Milton's lines convey the pain of smothering more than any other passage of poetry, even though this impression does not seem to be entirely justified by the text itself. In fact, the closest reference to choking is constituted by the fact that the Devil enters the snake through its mouth

---

comments: "Either Keats had a long-standing interest in snakes, or he marked these passages when he was contemplating or writing a poem featuring a colourful, deceptive-serpent woman" (33). She is clearly inclined to the latter option, but, since *Paradise Lost* inspires a passage of *Hyperion* too, the former cannot be excluded.
141 The note is transcribed in Lau's diplomatic edition of Keats's copy of Milton (153).
142 See Allott's note at page 411 of her edition of Keats's poems.

(*Paradise Lost* IX 187–188), but there is no image as powerful and openly stifling as "Making slow way, with head and neck convulsed / From over-strainèd might" (*Hyperion* I 262–263). In this passage, Keats makes semantically more explicit the suffocating effect that has stricken him so much while reading Milton, but he also resorts to his same metrical pattern. In fact, line 262 of Book 1 of *Hyperion* begins with an initial inversion just like line 187 of Book IX of *Paradise Lost*, which also presents a falling inversion immediately after the caesura. These irregularities hinder the metrical free flowing of the passage precisely in the line where the Devil starts entering the snake's mouth, so that they can be interpreted as the metrical equivalent for choking. Initial inversions in particular appear rather often in Keats's passages where serpents are present[143], as will be seen. Therefore, although this metrical device was regularly and widely employed by Augustan poets[144], it is likely that Keats derived the idea of using it in association with snakes – and particularly in order to convey their suffocating quality – from Milton. The highest concentration of initial inversions is to be found in *Lamia*, where they are even more frequent than in Pope[145], and, thence, the influence of Augustan prosody on the poem is not sufficient to account for their high number.

As already seen, the association between pain, smothering and the serpent, which Keats finds in Milton, is bound to become central in Keats's representation of snakes as well. In Milton's lines, suffocation is less immediately evident also because it is of a different kind. It depends less on contractions of the neck, i. e. strangling, than on "confinement" (*Keats's Paradise Lost* 153). Satan is trapped in the snake's body until morning and obliged to "unwilling stillness" (153), whereas it is precisely the intruder's movement to be emphasised in *Hyperion*[146]. The feeling of confinement in a serpent's body, however, is not ignored by Keats. It is hinted at by Glaucus in Book 3 of Endymion, when he wishes to get rid of his "serpent-skin of woe" (240), and more interestingly in *Lamia* through the same metaphor of the snake's body as a prison[147] which Keats uses in his comment to Milton. Definitely, Keats finds in Milton a suggestion of the serpent's body as a

---

143 See, for instance, *Isabella* 190 and *Lamia* I 45, 49, 50, 115, 116, 149, 152, 294. Initial inversions abound in the episode of Glaucus in Book 3 of *Endymion* too (see lines 483, 489, 491, 501, 502), but they cannot be derived from Milton since Keats started carefully reading and marking his copy of *Paradise Lost* in the early months of 1818 (Lau 23). In fact, initial inversions have here different functions, as will be seen, and do not occur in association with the image of suffocation at lines 525–526.
144 Bate defines the initial inversion as "one of the most prominent single peculiarities in Augustan metre" (161).
145 The percentage of initially inverted feet in *Lamia* is 6 %, while Pope, the Augustan poet who had drawn more upon this device, does not exceed 5 % (Bate 162).
146 The description presents two expressions of motion: "Crept gradual, from the feet unto the crown" (Hyperion I 260) and "Making slow way" (262).
147 Lamia's reptile body is defined as "the serpent prison-house" (*Lamia* I 203).

constriction, and, as his comment shows, responds to it very actively by specifying the smothering aspect of this confinement. He goes further in his poetry, where the sense of suffocation related to snakes is conveyed through convulsed necks, whose contractions imply a constriction of the throat and, thus, an impediment to vocal expression[148]. Once again, the novel elements that Keats introduces compared to the source are those more evidently linked with a metapoetic interpretation.

In the end, Milton is undoubtedly the most important source as far as the physical description of snakes is concerned, since it provides the focus on their twisted forms, the metaphors of the serpent's body as labyrinth and prison, and, most of all, the sense of suffocation as well as a corresponding rhythmic pattern. Nevertheless, there is still one recurring feature of Keatsian snakes that cannot be found in Milton, that is, their hypnotic eyes. I have already pointed out that serpents' mesmeric powers were among the commonly held beliefs of Romantic naturalists, so that Keats must have been aware of them since the time of his medical apprenticeship. This same idea is exploited in another poetic text of the time that appears to be a more effective source for Keats once he chose to undertake a career as a poet. In 1816 Coleridge published his long narrative poem *Christabel*, which is usually considered to have inspired *Lamia*, as it deals with an ambiguous, seductive, serpent-like female character[149]. In *Lamia*, however, the protagonist's transformation from snake into woman is witnessed at the beginning of Keats's narration, whereas Geraldine reveals her serpentine nature only in the second part of the poem and precisely through the telling element of the hypnotic stare. The key passage is as follows:

> [Geraldine] looked askance at Christabel –
> Jesu, Maria, shield her well!
> A snake's small eye blinks dull and shy;
> And the lady's eyes they shrunk in her head,
> Each shrunk up to a serpent's eye,
> And with somewhat malice, and more of dread,
> At Christabel she looked askance! –
> One moment – and the sight was fled!
> But Christabel in dizzy trance
> Stumbling on the unsteady ground
> Shuddered aloud, with a hissing sound. (*Christabel* 581-590)

---

148 In his article "Keats, Empathy, and the 'Poetic Character'", Ford interprets Keats's marginal note in almost opposite terms and precisely as a description of the action of empathy which allows Satan to enter into the snake (482-483). Yet he does not account for the emphasis on suffocation and pain, which are not found in Keats's descriptions of empathetic experiences, such as those linked to the negative capability. Ford himself admits that "the evidence is not sufficient to prove" (483) this association.

149 See Routh 33-37 and Stillinger 50-51.

Geraldine seems to undergo a partial, temporary metamorphosis, since her eyes turn from "large bright eyes" (574), which she casts down "in maiden wise" (573), into snake's ones, which make Christabel fall into a trance. What is more, Geraldine's spell works explicitly through "unconscious sympathy" (609), as it is typical of magic. Its first effect on Christabel is making her hiss[150], which means that she mimics both Geraldine's serpentine nature and her previous spell[151]. As a matter of fact, Geraldine's charm seems to affect Christabel so that she mimics it. It is even more evident as far as the mesmeric stare is concerned. Geraldine hypnotises Christabel through her serpent-like eyes, and, as a result, the tranced girl cannot but reproduce Geraldine's gaze because of the sympathetic bond the spell created between them:

> The maid, devoid of guile and sin,
> I know not how, in fearful wise,
> So deeply had she drunken in
> That look, those shrunken serpent eyes,
> That all her features were resigned
> To this sole image in her mind:
> And passively did imitate
> That look of dull and treacherous hate!
> And thus she stood, in dizzy trance,
> Still picturing that look askance
> With forced unconscious sympathy. (*Christabel* 599–609)

Coleridge makes more explicit a dynamics that Keats will represent in *Lamia* too. Just as Christabel is so conquered by Geraldine's spell that she is forced to imitate her, so Lycius is so enthralled by Lamia's bright eyes that his life is completely dependent on hers[152]. Furthermore, bright eyes are another element that Geraldine[153] and Lamia share, and this confirms their seductive, hypnotic powers[154].

---

150 Christabel had already emitted a hissing sound, when she saw her father embracing Geraldine, and had had a terrifying vision (459: "drew in her breath with a hissing sound"). Although Geraldine had not yet revealed as a serpent, the hiss was the effect of her spell, which prevented Christabel from telling her fear (473–474: "she had no power to tell / Aught else: so mighty was the spell"). It is noteworthy that the hiss is caused by an obstacle to her possibilities of expression, a theme which has been found in Keats. Moreover, it already has an implicit sympathetic nature, as Christabel mimics the way Geraldine casted her spell (247–248: "*drawing in her breath* [italics added] aloud, / Like one that shuddered").

151 In this case, it is the shuddering element that recurs: "Like one that shuddered" (248) is echoed in "Shuddered aloud" (590).

152 "With brighter eyes and slow amenity, / Put her new lips to his, and gave afresh / The life she had so tangled in her mesh" (*Lamia* I 293–295). It is noteworthy that Lycius's condition is defined as a "trance" (296), just like Christabel's one, in the following line.

153 Coleridge insists on Geraldine's brightness, in particular on her bright eyes: "a damsel bright" (*Christabel* 58), "her fair large eyes 'gan glitter bright" (221; 'fair' in Keats, as already

Even if, in the passage that has already been analysed, they seem to be contrasted with the serpent's dull eyes, they are actually equally mesmeric, as is proven by their acting on Sir Leoline[155]. A dazzling brightness also helps to identify Geraldine with the serpent in the bard's dream, which is presented as "a bright green snake / Coiled around its [a dove's] wings and neck"[156] (*Christabel* 549–550). Lamia's similar lustrous appearance has been already pointed out, although she is richer in colours and patterns, but it is also important to note that the serpent is here choking the dove by "Swelling its neck as she swelled hers" (554). The vision conveys an image of suffocation through strangling that is typical of snakes, even if not of Keatsian ones. Keats is probably more impressed by the swelling of the serpent's neck, which is reproduced by the dove according to the same mimetic bound produced by Geraldine's spell, and which reminds of the bloating would-be-Python in Book 3 of *Endymion* (525–526). Line 554 of *Christabel* is further noteworthy because it begins with a metrical initial inversion, so that reading Coleridge may have reinforced the association between this distortion of metrical regularity, which disturbs the flowing of reading, and the suffocating – both in the transitive and intransitive sense of the term – serpent that Keats found in Milton. Moreover, the same metrical pattern is repeated in the mentioned line 590, where, even if choking is not mentioned, Coleridge refers to the snake's hissing, that is, to a dysphoric sound that is produced by partially impeding the flow of air through the vocal tract.

Returning to the bright eyes, Keats is probably inspired also by another text by Coleridge where their mesmeric quality is made even more explicit, though not associated with snakes. In "The Rime of the Ancient Mariner" (1798), in fact, the "bright-eyed Mariner" (20, 40) holds the wedding guest "with his glittering eye" (13), so that "He cannot choose but hear" (18, 38). The importance of mentioning this poem too lies in the fact that hypnotism has here more clearly metapoetic implications, as the mariner exerts his control on the wedding guest just as long as he tells his story. The compelling power of words is added to that of the eyes, but these words are both the mariner's and the narrator's, so that they act, at the same time, on the guest and on the reader. Coleridge draws, thus, a parallel between the two levels of storytelling in order to render his poem itself a

---

seen, often refers to human hypnotic eyes, such as in *Lamia* I 63 and *Otho the Great* V ii 37), "Casting down her large bright eyes" (574), "She rolled her large bright eyes" (595).

154 As already seen, in "To My Brother George", the "bright glance" (15) possesses a beguiling power too, even if that of inspiration.

155 "She rolled her large bright eyes divine / Wildly on Sir Leoline" (*Christabel* 595–596; where 'divine' indicates Geraldine's supernatural nature).

156 Coleridge replays the archetypal opposition between snakes and birds.

work of poetic mesmerism, a result that is achieved through the contribution of rhythm and rhyme as well[157].

In conclusion, Keats resorts mainly to two groups of sources as far as the physical features of the serpent are concerned. On one hand, he relies on a Romantic predecessor, Coleridge, for the hypnotic eyes and the enticement through sympathy, both of which have a parallel in the Romantic conception of creativity, that is, the mesmeric quality of inspiration on the poet as well as of poetry on the reader, and the sympathetic communication of the poet's vision to his public, respectively. On the other hand, he finds in Milton elements that belong to a different isotopy, namely the contortion of forms or the suffocation caused by confinement. Both, however, convey a sort of difficulty or impediment, which, according to my metapoetic interpretation, can be led back to the effort at verbalising the poet's insight. The problem does not belong to the Romantic myth of creation or to its insistence on sympathy, so that, not by chance, Keats resorts to an author of the 17th century to represent it. Thus, the two groups of sources, and the corresponding characteristics of the snake that they suggest to Keats, reproduce the opposition between the two main attitudes to the problem of poetic verbalisation that constitute the 'living symbol' of the serpent.

---

157 On the link between "The Rime of the Ancient Mariner", mesmerism and poetic fascination, see Baumbach 135-143. A parallel between the serpent's hypnotic eye and the poet's fascinating power in Colerdige's works is detected in Pedrini 32-33 too, where it is written that "Even the poet himself felt the power of his own eye, which could rivet the attention of the listener and render him oblivious to all other aspects of the charmer" (32-33).

4. Textual analyses

4.1 *Endymion*

After analysing the main characteristics of the serpent throughout Keats's poetic production and defining the frame of reference for its metapoetic interpretation, I will now apply these notions to the passages that contain the most frequent and significant occurrences of snakes. The first peak of serpent symbolism is undoubtedly found in Book 3 of *Endymion* (September 1817), in particular in the episode of Glaucus and Circe, where three different snakes are present. Serpents had previously appeared only in Book 2 of *Endymion*, where they are interestingly linked with the awful visions Endymion sees after being left alone by Cynthia: "out he strayed / Half seeing visions that might have dismayed / Alecto's serpents" (873–875). 'Straying' corresponds to 'roaming' and, thus, Endymion's movement and his heightened state of consciousness[158] are akin to the wandering activity of imagination, as confirmed by the arising of visions. The fact that serpents are mentioned in conjunction with the visionary faculty is meaningful, yet their relationship is still embryonic.

Book 3 of *Endymion* is set in the undersea world, where the protagonist meets an old man who turns out to be Glaucus. After welcoming Endymion as a saviour, he tells him how he was cursed to a life of unending ageing at the bottom of the sea by Circe and how Endymion was prophesied to be the one to free him. The central part of the story revolves around the time Glaucus spends on the island of Circe, to whom he resorts in order to find a remedy to his unrequited love for Scylla. Yet, instead of helping him, Circe herself falls in love with him and magically seduces him, so that he is bound to stay with her in her realm of sensual pleasure. The moment when Glaucus finally discovers that Circe allures men to turn them into beasts corresponds also to the passage where serpent symbolism is concentrated. As one morning Glaucus wakes alone, he falls prey

---

158 See lines 875–877: "ravishments more keen / Than Hermes' pipe, when anxious he did lean / Over eclipsing eyes".

to discomfort and looks for Circe in the forest until he comes to "a dark valley" (*Endymion* III 490).

> Groanings swelled
> Poisonous about my ears, and louder grew
> The nearer I approached a flame's gaunt blue
> That glared before me through a thorny brake.
> This fire, like the eye of gordian snake,
> Bewitched me towards, and I soon was near
> A sight too fearful for the feel of fear. (490-496)

What Glaucus sees are precisely the men Circe turned into animals and the display of their disturbing animality, yet, before dealing with them, I will focus on the very significant and ambiguous element of the blue flame. The fire that suddenly appears to Glaucus has been usually interpreted as a magical emanation of Circe and, thus, negatively connoted. Lura and Duilio Pedrini, for instance, consider the whole passage as a description of "Circe's evil powers", in particular "her exercising her serpent wiles upon the forest shapes" (99), as if the eye-like fire were Circe's means to hypnotise the creatures in the wood[159]. It is undoubted that there is a link between the enchantress and the flame, since they share some characteristics, such as a bewitching power[160], a related magical nature, and a glaring appearance[161]. If the role of the fire is considered on an actantial level, however, it becomes clear that it opposes Circe rather than act according to her will. The flame, in fact, leads Glaucus to the "haggard scene" (497) which allows him to discover the truth about Circe by showing him the fate that befalls her victims. Without the guidance of the blue fire, he would have remained at the mercy of her seductive spell and unable to acknowledge the "real hell" hidden behind the semblance of "specious heaven" (476). Therefore, even if the atmosphere of the whole scene is rather disquieting, and the flame itself is "gaunt" (492), i.e. somewhat gloomy, it actually plays a positive role in the development of the episode and works as a narrative hinge. In addition, the compresence of opposite axiological connotations – in this case, the Circean nature of the serpentine fire and its revealing function – immediately suggests its

---

159 Other examples of authors who consider the flame as Circe's fire are De Almeida (187) and Aske (129).
160 Being an "enchantress" (*Endymion* III 413), she addresses Glaucus with "charming syllables" (444), while the flame "bewitche[s]" (495) him.
161 The flame "glare[s]" (493) in front of Glaucus, while Circe metaphorically "flashe[s]" (412) across his mind as a possible solution to his lovesickness, and, as a consequence, he decides to look for her. When he then tries to flee from her, she sharply appears in front of him: "I fled three days – when lo! before me stood / *Glaring* [italics added] the angry witch" (566-567).

identification as 'living symbol', which will be further confirmed during the present analysis.

If on an actantial level the appearance of the blue flame breaks the narrative stalemate by leading Glaucus to the discovery of truth, the latter is achieved not through the rational analysis of clues or deduction, but through a magic revelation. Glaucus does not *understand* Circe's secret, but he rather *sees* it, which has important consequences on the interpretation, if another level of the text – that is, the metapoetic one – is taken into account. The activation of this level is signalled by some key elements at the beginning of the narrative sequence, which should be familiar by now. When Glaucus awakes and finds out that Circe is missing from his side, he starts searching the forest "Wandering about in pine and cedar gloom" (483), where 'wandering' is the verb of Romantic imagination par excellence. The ramblings of Glaucus parallel the activity of the mind during divergent thinking, as is proven by his heightened state of consciousness as well. Glaucus proceeds as if in trance: "I stumbled / Down a precipitous path as if impelled" (488–489). He does not seem to control his actions but to be guided by some other mysterious power, as happens to the mind when it is dominated by an unconscious principle and, in line with the Romantic view of artistic creation, by imagination. The idea of the unconscious is suggested also by the setting in the forest itself and by the presence of darkness in spite of the early hour (467: "haunts umbrageous"; 490: "dark valley"), elements which are both archetypically associated with the unconscious[162]. In addition, the dimness of the place is confirmed on a phonosymbolic level by the predominance of back vowels – such as [u, ʊ, o, ʌ, ɔ, ɒ] – in the descriptive sequences about the forest[163]. According to Tsur, not only are back vowels perceived as darker, but their acoustic signal is also marked by "relatively low differentiation" (23)[164], a characteristic that suits well the undifferentiated nature of the unconscious[165]. This is also the probable reason why the glaring of the flame is "gaunt" (492): its light does not belong to the daylight realm of consciousness but possesses, instead, a ghastly hue.

---

162 Jung deals with both: "The *forest* is a symbol of the unconscious" (Jung, *Children's Dreams* 262); "Day and light are synonyms for consciousness, night and dark for the unconscious" (Jung, *The Archetypes and the Collective Unconscious* 167).
163 Back vowels – with the addition of the undifferentiated semivowel [w] – are underlined in the following lines: "When I awoke, 'twas in a twilight bower, / Just when the light of morn, with hum of bees, / Stole through its verdurous matting of fresh trees" (418–420); "And I was free of haunts umbrageous, / Could wander in the mazy forest-house / Of squirrels, foxes shy, and antlered deer, / And birds from coverts innermost, and drear / Warbling for very joy mellifluous sorrow" (467–471).
164 For an analysis of the darker, less differentiated aspect of back vowels, see Tsur 20-25.
165 "Everything unconscious is undifferentiated, and everything that happens unconsciously proceeds on the basis of non-differentiation" (Jung, *Two Essays in Analytical Psychology* 206).

The blue colour of the flame is meaningful as well. Vivian and Wilhelmina Jakobs erroneously ascribe it to an English tradition of devilish blue, due to their negative opinion on its axiological value (39), yet they also highlight its important relationship with magic by asserting that "the blue flame was a necessary accompaniment of the magic act" (40)[166]. In addition, blue is more often associated with heaven, that is, with the deity and, in a non-religious worldview, with supernatural beings. Keats himself regularly depicts heaven – not in the banal sense of sky but to indicate an unworldly region – as blue[167], so that the colour of the flame depends on its coming from an extrahuman dimension, which is precisely the same as imagination's. In the chapter about Keats's conception of creativity, the heavenly origin of imagination has been stressed as a means to represent its unconscious quality. The same idea is conveyed through the cold aspect of colour blue. According to the famous theory of colour by Kandinsky[168], in fact, "warmth or cold in a colour means an approach respectively to yellow or to blue" (80), and the temperature affects the observer in different ways: "the warm colours approaching the spectator, the cold ones retreating from him" (*ibidem*). Being the coldest of colours, blue conveys the greatest sense of distance as well, so that it is perfectly suited to represent the ontological gap between our world and the supernatural one.

All these elements lead to an identification of the blue flame with something that sharply arises from the unconscious through the activation of the wandering imagination, as is proven by the comparison with the serpent, which has been previously related to the emergence of the imaginative insight to consciousness. It will be now seen whether the serpentine nature of the fire, which has been so far neglected, confirms the paradigm of interpretation I have been applying. The flame is related to a snake due to three characteristics of the latter: its unexpected appearance, its hypnotic eyes, and its twisted shape. The first two elements can

---

166 Glaucus's magic cloak is blue: "A cloak of blue wrapped up his aged bones, / O'erwrought with symbols by the deepest groans / Of ambitious magic" (*Endymion* III 197–199).

167 See some examples of the association of blue with a supernatural dimension in works preceding Book 3 of *Endymion:* "the *blue* [italics added] dwelling of divine Urania" ("To Charles Cowden Clarke", 41); "Ah, see her hovering feet, / More *bluely* [italics added] veined, more soft, more whitely sweet / Than those of sea-born Venus" (*Endymion* I 624–626); "Her scarf into a fluttering pavilion; / 'Tis *blue* [italics added]" (628–629; blue appears to be Cynthia's colour); "O Cynthia, ten-times bright and fair! / From thy *blue* [italics added] throne" (II 170–171). Keats interestingly explicitly links the blue with the unconscious dimension of poetic creation in "To My Brother George". Firstly, he compares his lack of inspiration with the inability to catch the music of the spheres, i. e. an otherworldly melody, though he looks into the deep, i. e. in the unconscious: "No sphery strains by me could e'er be caught / From the *blue* [italics added] dome, though I to dimness gaze / On the far depth where sheeted lighting plays" (4–6). Secondly, the tranced poet is depicted as one able to see "The revelries and mysteries of night" (64) in "the dark, silent blue" (57).

168 Kandinsky too acknowledges that "Blue is the typical heavenly colour" (83).

be taken into account together. The fire recalls a serpent's eye mainly because of its mesmerising power; in fact, it "bewitche[s]" Glaucus "towards" (495), that is, it guides him, but also compels him to go forwards. It is, therefore, revealed to be akin to the mysterious force that "impelled" (489) him before. They both affect him in ways that are beyond his control, like the arising of unconscious imagination according to the Romantic conception of creativity. It has been said that the serpent does not represent the unconscious – or, in this case, the imagination – as a whole, but more specifically their manifestation to consciousness. The glaring of the flame can be interpreted in this way, because, though its light is "gaunt" (492), it is still a light and, thus, tending towards consciousness. Moreover, its brightness belongs to the isotopy of hypnotism typical of Keats, but it also conveys the idea of revelation as a metaphorical illumination. As already hinted at, the truth strikes Glaucus as an epiphany. The knowledge he acquires through the flame is intuitive, unmediated by rational or analytical processes. On a metapoetic level, it corresponds to the moment of the imaginative insight, which, as already seen, has precisely a mesmeric effect on the poet's consciousness.

The idea of a truth – be it the truth of Circe's nature or that of the imaginative insight – that is not acquired through the linear processes of convergent thinking is confirmed by the other element that associates the serpent with the flame, that is, its "gordian" (494) shape. The serpentine intricacy is paralleled by the "thorny brake" (493), through which the fire appears to Glaucus, but also by the "mazy forest-house" of Circe's island, where Glaucus "Could wander" (468). These two declinations of tortuosity are partly different. The latter corresponds to the "wandering" (483) movement that leads Glaucus to the fire and that represents the mind's divergent way of getting to the imaginative insight. Its importance is stressed by the metrical inversion, which ensures that "wandering" is pronounced with the accent on the first syllable, even if it is at the beginning of an iambic pentameter.

Circe's forest is the dark place where the only possible way of proceeding is wandering. It is a mental place dominated by symmetrical logic, where the succession of time is annihilated, and opposite moments of the day coexist: "When I awoke, 'twas in a *twilight* [italics added] bower, / Just when the light of *morn* [italics added], with hum of bees, / Stole through its verdurous matting of fresh trees" (418–419). As already said, it is dominated by dark, undifferentiated vowels but also by voiceless fricatives[169], which have been previously identified

---

169 Voiceless fricatives carry more weight when they are found at the beginning of words that are semantically charged and metrically stressed – such as "free", "haunts" (467), "forest", "house" (468), "squirrels", "foxes", "shy" (469) – or at the end of the line in syllables with a beat – such as "umbrageous" (467) and "house" (468). Voiceless fricatives return in pro-

with animal noise, and, not by chance, it is in these same lines 467–471 that the animal inhabitants of the forest are mentioned. Since voiceless sounds are nearer to the inarticulate, they help to convey the preverbal nature of unconscious insights. Returning to the labyrinth as an image of the non-linear processes of divergent thinking, the unpredictable course of Glaucus's roaming is also conveyed through metrical irregularities, which act as if to twist the metrical pattern. For instance, line 487 presents a strong falling inversion without virtual offbeat at the end, so that "earth-thunder" receives two consecutive beats on the first syllables[170], while line 489 starts with the initial inversion of "Down a precipitous", which gives a corresponding sense of acceleration[171]. The same pattern is found at the beginning of line 491, which immediately precedes the apparition of the flame, whereas, in the previous line, the rhythm suddenly slows down when it comes to the "dark valley" (490) due to another falling inversion without virtual offbeat that produces two consecutive beats. The metre seems thus to follow Glaucus in his irregular, non-linear wandering and becomes regular again from line 492 onward after the apparition of the fire.

To sum up, the magic flame that resembles a snake's eye symbolises the unexpected manifestation of the imaginative insight to consciousness. The isotopy of tortuosity corresponds to the divergent way of thinking that dominates the unconscious mind as well as to the intricacies of poetic imagination, according to a metaphor that was particularly dear to Keats in this period[172]. In addition, the hypnotic glaring of the fire reinforces the idea of an intuitive, non-rational epiphany and of the overwhelming effect of inspiration, which takes control of the poet despite his own will. This whole set of ideas clearly belongs to the Romantic conception of creativity, which Keats seems here to share completely. However, another aspect of the symbolism of this image emerges if the "thorny brake" (493) is taken into account. This intricate vegetation may be interpreted as a further representation of the labyrinthine path of the imaginative faculty, yet its function is not the same, since it follows the apparition of the serpentine flame, i. e. the insight, rather than indicate the process that leads Glaucus to it. Conversely, it is something that comes between him and the fire, almost as an obstacle. The flame glares *through* the brake, that is, the light must pass through a narrow, intricate passage in order to reach Glaucus and bring its

---

minent position a few lines below, where the hellish nature of the place is mentioned, and they appear at the beginning of key words: "<u>s</u>pecious", "<u>h</u>eaven" and "<u>h</u>ell" (476).

170 "When a falling inversion without a virtual offbeat is used, there is a distinct increase in *tension*, as the rhythm of the words *pulls away from* [italics added] the expected metrical pattern" (Attridge 118).
171 The perception of an acceleration in the rhythm is further emphasised by the fact that "precipitous" (489) needs to be pronounced in three syllables instead of four.
172 See at least "On Receiving a Laurel Crown from Leigh Hunt" (3), which was written a few months before, in April 1817.

revelation to him. Another level can thus be added to the interpretation, which still belongs to a metapoetic paradigm, but deals with the communication of the insight rather than with its manifestation to the poet's mind. If the fire's purpose is to reveal Circe's true nature to Glaucus, in fact, it somehow relates to Glaucus in terms of communication. Therefore, the blue light that is filtered by the brake is isomorphic to the imaginative insight that is conveyed to the reader through the dull signs of language[173].

The theme is here only hinted at and not fully developed yet, as direct references to vocal emission lack. It is, however, suggested by phonosymbolism, since the dazzle of the flame is marked by consonant clusters, which are underlined in the following lines: "The nearer I approached a flame's gaunt blue / That glared before me through a thorny brake" (492–493). Apart from [fl], the other clusters are formed by plosives and liquids. Since the vocal tract is blocked during the articulation of plosives, while liquids are continuous phonemes, their succession conveys the idea of a sound that has to pass through a blocked passage before being finally released. It is also important to note that this obstruction is not total yet, as the plosives are mainly voiced, which means that some air makes the vocal cords vibrate. The dynamics of constraint and release is continued through the diphthongs that follow the clusters and are, in their turn, followed by voiceless plosives. Since diphthongs correspond to an extension of the continuous vocalic sound, they make the successive obstruction more marked, such as in "approached" (492), where [əʊ] precedes [tʃt][174], or "brake" (493), where [eɪ] is followed by [k][175]. This continuous alternation of blocking and releasing patterns represents the strain of vocal emission and, similarly, the difficulty of communicating the insight to the reader through the narrowing, somewhat painful[176] filter of language.

Keats seems to raise the issue of poetic verbalisation, but his solution still conforms to Romantic principles. If it is true that the analysed lines end with [k], which, as will be seen, is the most suffocating phoneme and, therefore, will become more important in *Hyperion*, voiceless velar plosives are present also in

---

173 See, for instance, the sonnet "When I have fears that I may cease to be" (21–31 January 1816), where the poet's aim corresponds to tracing the "shadows" (8) of the "Huge cloudy symbols" (6) of his vision. Words are nothing but shadows of the contents of imagination. Moreover, poetic composition is here described as dominated by the unconscious faculty as the poet traces these signs "with the magic hand of chance" (8).
174 The succession of affricate and plosive intensifies the blocking effect since the affricate itself begins with a plosive and releases as a fricative.
175 See also "gaunt" (492), which begins with voiced plosive followed by the long vowel [ɔː] and ends with a voiceless plosive, or "glared" (493), where the initial cluster precedes [ɛə] and the final [d].
176 Both the blocked vocal tract and the "thorny" (493) quality of the brake suggest the isotopy of pain.

the following line in "like" (494) and, above all, in "snake" (494), which not only is the key word of the present analysis, but it is also placed in the final stressed position. The appearance of this phoneme together with the serpent is a further proof of the association between the snake and a hindrance in the process of communication of the insight, a hindrance that, however, is not here unsurmountable. The obstacle of the thorny brake is eventually overcome, and overcome in a Romantic way, that is, through the hypnotic power of the snake's eye. The twofoldness of poetic mesmerism can be found here, since it applies both to the effect of the insight on the poet and to the action of poetry on the reader. As already said, the flame communicates to Glaucus through revelation and through the intuitive, sympathetic mode of magic. The flame does not *tell* him the truth, but rather *shows* him a "sight" (496), that is, it conveys the vision to Glaucus.

However, when the sight itself is taken into account, there are some other interesting elements that seem to partly problematise the Romantic view, and that coincide with the apparition of serpents. First of all, the scene that Glaucus spectates is dominated by chaotic animality. 'Serpent' is turned into a verb that indicates anarchic motion in line 501 ("Laughing, and wailing, grovelling, serpenting"), where the accumulation of present participles conveys a sense of overwhelming dynamism[177]. As reiterated, inhuman animation usually symbolises the preverbal, prelogical nature of the contents of the unconscious, which elude human grasp. It thus hints at the visionary realm of unconscious imagination, as further proven by the fragmented syntax of line 501. The sequence of present participles, where only the first two are logically connected through a conjunction, conveys the idea of a vision that occurs in a state of altered consciousness and perceives the discrete elements of reality without organising them in a coherent, logical unity. Furthermore, the whole scene is dominated by inarticulate, dysphoric noise: from the semantic chiasm that intertwines sound and pain in line 485 ("A sound of agony, an agony of sound") to the "earth-thunder"[178] (487), the poisonous "Groanings" (490) and the "wailing" (501). The most deafening explosion of animal noise, however, occurs after Circe casts her spell on her "brute" (500) victims:

> Whereat was heard a noise of painful toil,
> Increasing gradual to a tempest rage,
> Shrieks, yells, and groans of torture-pilgrimage,
> Until their grieved bodies 'gan to bloat
> And puff from the tail's end to stifled throat.

---

[177] Present participles as epithets convey the dynamic sense of unrestrained flowing, as shown by their opposition with past participles (see Bate 96, 148–149).
[178] Its explosiveness is stressed by the succession of two beats on the first two syllables.

> Then was appalling silence, then a sight
> More wildering than all that hoarse affright,
> For the whole herd, as by a whirlwind writhen,
> Went through the dismal air like one huge Python
> Antagonizing Boreas – and so vanished. (522-531)

The importance of the passage as the first occurrence of the theme of suffocation – even if only indirectly referred to a snake – has already been stressed, but some remarks need to be added. Due to Circe's magic, a transformation befalls the animals through a process that is divided into two equally long phases: in the first (522-526) their bodies inflate, while in the second (527-531) they form a huge serpent in the air and disappear. The two moments differ also in sounds, since the first is dominated by the screams of the beasts in pain, whereas the second by a sudden silence – a bipartition which is echoed on a phonosymbolic level. Plosives and clusters with plosives abound in lines 522-526, especially in prominent positions, such as in stressed syllables at the beginning or end of words[179]. Plosives are articulated by blocking the vocal tract, while clusters that are composed of a succession of plosives and liquids, as seen above, convey the idea of a blocked sound that is released with difficulty. By contrast, the cluster [st] corresponds to the highest degree of obstruction, as a continuous sound ends with a voiceless plosive. It is found at the end of "tempest" (523), which defines the cacophonous struggle of the beasts, and, above all, at the beginning of "stifled" (526), the key word of the isotopy of suffocation, where the cluster carries more weight, since it is found in the initial, stressed syllable of the word. Even though the following diphthong [aɪ] prolongs the vocal emission and seems to suggest a release after the blocking cluster, "throat" almost reverses the pattern. The diphthong [əʊ] precedes the voiceless dental plosive [t] in the last stressed syllable of the line, so that the sense of obstruction is eventually confirmed as well as reinforced. As a matter of fact, the phonic patterns of these lines seem to express a sense of suffocation rather than distressed screams, so that this element turns out to be predominant.

From line 526 the prevalent phonic pattern of the passage changes, as the metrical stressed positions do not coincide with the presence of plosives to the same extent as in the previous lines. The sudden silence that follows the mention of suffocation seems to be onomatopoeically rendered through the recurring of the [h] in stressed syllables, which can be considered as the most silent phoneme. Voiceless glottal fricatives become particularly significant in line 529, where they are found at the beginning of two consecutive stressed syllables ("whole herd")

---

179 See "Whereat", "heard", "painful", "toil" (522), "Increasing", "gradual", "tempest" (523), "Shrieks", "groans", "torture-pilgrimage" (524), "Until", "grieved", "bodies", "gan", "bloat" (525), "puff", "tail's", "end", "stifled", "throat" (526).

due to a rising inversion. After an initial acceleration, in fact, the sequence of two beats makes the rhythm slow down, so that the voiceless glottal fricatives turn out to be greatly emphasised. This marked metrical irregularity occurs together with the apparition of the animals in the form of Python, that is, with the representation of the struggle the vision undergoes in order to materialise in our world[180]. The vision, indeed, is not verbal yet and still belongs to the realm of the inarticulate, as is proven by the concentration of voiceless fricatives – not only the [h] but also [s] and [f] – in metrically preeminent positions[181]. The metapoetic interpretation of the serpent formed by other animals as the vision during the strenuous act of its own communication is justified by the focus on stifled throats, i. e. the organ that is most immediately associated with the emission of voice, as well as by the phonosymbolic insistence on phonemes that are marked by total or partial obstruction of the vocal tract.

The perception of a difficulty in turning the divergent insight into convergent words does not belong to the Romantic conception of creativity, according to which the gap between the two can be bridged through unmediated sympathy, which metaphorically corresponds to the mode of magic and, therefore, to the preceding image of the flame. In order to avoid misunderstanding, I should make clear that the problem of verbalisation is still present in an embryonic form in *Endymion*. The elements that point at this metapoetic interpretation and that have been mentioned in the previous paragraph, in fact, do not yet form the coherent isotopy that will be found later. It is in *Hyperion* that the serpent, the obstruction of the vocal tract, and poetic communication really come together through the mediation of convulsion. In the passage that has just been analysed, instead, these elements work more as suggestions. Phonemes that are produced by somewhat blocking the air stream are prominent, but suffocation is the effect of inflating rather than convulsion, which better corresponds to the difficulty of vocal emission by contraction. In addition, the focus on the throat is present but not directly referred to the serpent. Similarly, the plosives precede its appearance, so that the snake does not seem to actually symbolise a hindrance yet.

Furthermore, the overall predominance of the Romantic paradigm as frame of reference is made clear by taking into account the other serpent that is present in Book 3 of *Endymion*. The serpentine flame has been said to play a positive role

---

180 Vanishing is more clearly interpreted as a passage from a world to another or a change in ontological condition in *Lamia*, where she disappears in the moment she turns into a woman (I 166).

181 See "silence", "sight" (527), "hoarse", "affright" (528), but this pattern returns also a few lines below, mostly in words that refer to the supernatural, animal or hybrid creatures of Circe's realm, which confirms their association with the inarticulate: see "phantoms" (533), "fauns", "nymphs", "satyrs", "stark" (534), "Swifter", "centaurs" (536), "Sighing", "elephant" (537), "Before", "fierce" (538) and "human" (539).

in the narrative development of the episode, since it allows Glaucus to unveil Circe's deceit, but it is only partly true in a longer-term perspective. As an immediate result of his discovery, Glaucus is cursed by Circe to a life of unending ageing (570–600). At the beginning of his tale, his pitiful condition is compared with a serpent-skin (238–240: "O shell-borne Neptune, I am pierced and stung / With new-born life! What shall I do? Where go / When I have cast this serpent-skin of woe?"), which is an image both of confinement and potential rebirth. This return to life, however, can be achieved only through the magic intervention of Endymion[182], which is interestingly accompanied by music.

As soon as he starts performing the spell, "Sweet music" (767) is heard and the whole scene is dominated by euphoric sounds: "A noise of harmony" (791), "Delicious symphonies, like airy flowers" (798) and "unseen leaves of sounds divine" (800). The imagery of vegetal growth stands for the free-flowing aspect of this music, but it is also a very common Romantic metaphor for the spontaneity of artistic creation, which is familiar to Keats too[183]. As a matter of fact, magic, musicality and natural growth are all elements that have been seen to metaphorically distinguish poetry – in particular, its more Romantic conception – in Keats's works. Their confluence in this passage makes it possible to conjecture the presence of a metapoetic level, according to which an outburst of spontaneous poetry is the only way to free Glaucus from the painful confinement of the serpent-skin. The latter seems to symbolise a static impasse when compared to the other images of animal dynamism, which have been identified with the visionary vitality of the unconscious. Just as what moves is alive, so Glaucus's blocked condition is precisely equated to a state of non-life, but one dominated by woe. As already seen, pain is constantly associated with snakes and is present in both the passage of the fire through the thorny brake and the formation of the Python. If it is true that they both somehow suggest the transformation of vision into words, Glaucus's confinement in the skin corresponds to a moment of painful impasse because of the momentary impossibility to achieve this passage. It is the stasis of the in-between moment before the liberation thanks to the music of poetry[184].

In conclusion, the episode of Glaucus and Circe is undoubtedly one of the most important moments of serpent symbolism in the entire production of Keats's poems. Different snakes come one after the other and seem to work as a Chinese box. The serpentine flame reveals to Glaucus that Circe turns her victim into beasts, which, in their turn, struggle to form a huge Python into the air and

---

182 He also puts on Glaucus's "dark blue cloak" (751) in order to perform the magic.
183 See *Letters*, vol. 1, 238–239.
184 Glaucus's return to life and movement is marked by a concentration of dynamic adjectives in -ing: "ravishing" (772), "lightning" (775), "Smiling" (776), "Out-sparkling" (777), "stepping" (778).

vanish. The discovery leads Glaucus to be cursed by Circe, a condition that he compares to being trapped in a serpent-skin, until the freeing intervention of Endymion. Serpents continuously appear, but they are never the same, also as far as their metapoetic interpretation is concerned. The fire represents the manifestation of the divergent insight to consciousness but also its communication through the immediacy of revelation, while the Python insists on the struggle of the vision to form and, possibly, to become concrete through words. The serpent-skin suggests the confinement in an impasse that is resolved by a spontaneous overflow of poetry. It is hence evident the dynamism of the serpent as a symbol, whose meaning constantly shifts – even if inside a common paradigm that revolves around imagination and poetic communication –, so that something which the serpent stands for or substitutes cannot be identified. Rather, its appearance indicates the emergence of a set of intertwined poetic problems, which revolves around the contrast between the spontaneity of the arising of the imaginative insight as well as the immediacy of its communication – conveyed through the isotopies of magic, hypnotism and musicality – and the difficulties of turning visions into words – suggested through the isotopies of intricacy[185], suffocation and pain, which have not been fully developed yet. This opposition constitutes the tension between opposites that generates a 'living symbol', and, indeed, it is never completely resolved. Even if the first set of ideas has been shown to prevail in the episode as a whole, the second one continues to emerge precisely through the image of the snake.

I will now focus on the reason why the symbol of the serpent and the corresponding issue of poetic communication first appear to a great extent in Book 3 of *Endymion*, which is the poem of the triumph of imagination. In *Endymion*, every dream is an Adam's dream, which means that the outer realisation of the inner vision is guaranteed and basically unproblematic. The letter where Keats asserts his faith in the truth of imagination and coins the comparison with Adam's dream dates back to November 1817, shortly after the composition of Book 3 of *Endymion*, yet it does not present any of the concerns about the risks of unbound imagination, which have been previously linked with an awareness of the restrictions language imposes on vision. The question was first hinted at in the verse letter Keats sent to Reynolds on 25 March 1818. Therefore, Book 3 was written in a period when Keats had not yet questioned the Romantic idea of the unmediated, sympathetic communication of the poet's insights to the reader, and, indeed, it is musical magic that triumphs in the end[186].

---

185 Intricacy is an important symbol of the non-linear processes of imagination too, as seen in the paragraph about this poetic faculty and when dealing with the twisted shape of the serpent.
186 Bostetter argues that, at the time of *Endymion* and the letter about the authenticity of

However, there is another element of Romantic poetics that Keats had already questioned in a letter of the previous spring that he copied to Bailey on 8 October 1817. In this letter, which has been already analysed, Keats defends his choice of writing a long narrative poem instead of the short lyrical poems that are the typical Romantic genre. At the same time, he celebrates the poetic virtue of invention for the first and last time. Invention is a rational, convergent faculty that does not belong to the Romantic paradigm of creativity, so that it defies the Romantic myth of an entirely divergent process of creation.

The necessity of conscious, deliberate invention emerges when Keats deals with a long, narrative poem, which requires a more evident rational effort than lyric poetry, since the raw matter of the narration needs to be arranged on a temporal axis according to the principles of asymmetrical logic. The imposition of a chronological order works on the imaginative insight, which, instead, follows the rules of symmetrical logic, as a constriction. The problem is akin to that of verbalisation, which has been associated with the images of convulsed serpent, as the difficulties of turning the vision into language depend, precisely, on the sequential, convergent nature of the latter. The two issues are, thus, related. This is the reason why serpent symbolism is concentrated in narrative poems and appears for the first time in *Endymion*, whereas it is completely absent in earlier poetic compositions, which conform to the standard of Romantic lyric poetry[187]. Therefore, if it is true that the specific problem of the convergent nature of language arose later – indeed, the focus on vocal emission is not complete yet –, Keats was already aware of other restrictions that are imposed on the products of imagination through asymmetrical laws in order to turn them into a poem, in this case a narrative one. The letter about invention, which was written in spring, and then copied at the beginning of October, allows us to assume that Keats bore in mind this issue while composing Book 3 of *Endymion*.

There is still one question to answer, that is, the reason why serpent symbolism concentrates in the episode of Circe. The solution has to be found precisely in the figure of the enchantress. Circe seems to embody the fascinating power of poetry due to the insistence on the musicality of her voice, which entices Glaucus and does not seem to differ much from Endymion's final magic.

---

imagination, Keats "was so confident that the truth is spontaneously revealed in the imaginative experience" (363), as it happens to Glaucus through the blue flame, but he also underlines that Keats gradually came to doubt his conviction together with "the fundamental tenets of Romantic poetry" (371). The emphasis on Keats's questioning of the Romantic idea of intuitive knowledge and communication through imagination is important to the present analysis as well, but Bostetter outlines this process in a too simplistic way, as if it were linear, whereas Keats partly returns to Romantic principles after *Hyperion*, as Bostetter neglects to notice and will be seen talking of *Lamia*.

187 I have already quoted the numerous Romantic equations of poetry and singing that are found in Keats's early poetry.

She speaks "honey-words" (426) that create a "net whose thraldom was more bliss than all / The range of flowered Elysium"[188] (427–428). Her "rich speech" is "dew" (429), and she links "Her charming syllables, till indistinct / Their music came to [Glaucus's] o'er sweetened-sound" (443–445). Dew, honey, and sweetness are all elements that are associated with manna, that is, a substance deriving from heaven, but it should be remembered that Circe's realm is only a "specious heaven" that hides a "real hell" (476). Her seduction is dangerous, since it ensnares her victims in a sterile impasse. Just as the image of words as heavenly food and music suggests an identification with poetry, her realm is dominated by symmetrical laws and anarchic animality, that is, by the unbound potential of unconscious imagination. Caught in a stalemate, Glaucus cannot but wander in it until he spectates the pain and struggle of the beasts to exit this place, and he has to free himself from his "serpent-skin of woe" (240). In conclusion, Keats seems to confront the dangerous aspects of the seduction of poetry and the poetic necessity to bring the vision outside its unconscious, preverbal dimension by facing the obstacles and limitations of convergent thinking, but, in the end, he resolves the problem in line with a Romantic conception of creativity, be it through the magic revelation of the blue flame, or through the musical spell of Endymion. The idea of poetic communication as a magic and thus sympathetic as well as spontaneous act is still reaffirmed.

4.2 Serpents and birds

Just as Glaucus laments his pitiful present condition by resorting to the simile of the serpent (*Endymion* III 240), his happy previous state is compared with that of "a new fledge bird" (388) who tries his pinions. In this case, the opposition between the two animals is based on liberty, since the former represents confinement, whereas the latter possibility of unbound movement and "freedom" (391). The antithesis between snakes and birds, however, is far wider than its application in this passage, as it is regularly found on an archetypal level, as well as in the occurrences of animals throughout Keats's poetic production. I have already drawn the attention on the fact that the animals that occur more frequently than serpents are all birds. As this opposition works on archetypal – i.e., according to my perspective, cultural – and distributional levels, it should be asked what its meaning is in a metapoetic frame of reference. The occurrences of snakes have been noted to concentrate in the narrative poems, while they are completely absent from the odes of spring 1819, which can be considered as Keats's most important Romantic achievement. Conversely, the odes present

---

188 There is here the same vegetal imagery as in lines 798–800.

some mentions of birds[189], which, unsurprisingly, concentrate in "Ode to a Nightingale" (May 1819).

In this ode, the most important characteristic of the bird is, undoubtedly, its singing. Therefore, what will be here pointed out referring to the nightingale of the ode can be applied to most of Keats's birds, since they are often presented while singing[190]. The nightingale "sing[s] of summer in full-throated ease" (10), and the surrounding forest seems to be transformed by its music into a "melodious plot / Of beechen green" (8-9). The bird's singing is conveyed through the word 'ease', which means that it is effortless, spontaneous, and quite the opposite of the difficulties in vocal emission that distinguishes Keatsian snakes. At the same time, just as the serpent's hiss belongs to the dimension of dysphoric noise, the nightingale produces euphoric music, so that their vocal dimensions contrast on all sides. It has been pointed out that music, in particular singing, are usual metaphors that Keats uses in order to indicate poetry. It is thus clear that the nightingale is a poetic animal, and, what is more, it embodies a Romantic model of poetry. Romantic authors, in fact, believe in the necessary spontaneity of the act of composition. As Keats himself asserts, poetry must come "as naturally as the leaves to a tree" (*Letters*, vol. 1, 238). The poet's insight must be turned into a poem in an unmediated, instinctive way, which resembles the effortless, natural singing of the nightingale. Since birds, like snakes, belong to the animal reign, and their free flight can be compared to roaming[191], they may be related to the unconscious and, precisely, to the imagination, yet they represent a completely different perspective on the problem of verbalisation. As a matter of fact, birds symbolise the absence of a problematic dimension in this act in line with the Romantic conception. This is the reason why, even though *Endymion* belongs to a Romantic frame of reference and eventually resolves the

---

189 See "birds" ("Ode to Psyche" 56), "owl" ("Ode on Melancholy" 7), "throstle" ("Ode on Indolence" 48), "red-breast" ("To Autumn" 32), "swallows" (33).

190 The following examples refer only to the general term 'bird': "The songs of birds" ("How many bards gild the lapses of time" 10), "All the tenderest birds there [...] sing" ("Sleep and Poetry" 252, 254), "birds from coverts innermost and drear / Warbling" (*Endymion* III 470-471), "a fledgy sea-bird quire" ("Not Aladdin magian" 39), "Sweet birds antheming the morn" ("Fancy" 42), "no bird sing" ("La Belle Dame Sans Merci" 4, 48), "birds no sweet song" ("To [Fanny]" 42).

191 In "Fancy", Keats insists on the wandering movement of the poetic faculty, and, at the same time, attributes some features of a bird to it by calling it "winged" (5). Moreover, in "Sleep and Poetry", birds are also said to "creep" (253), which is a verb that has been found referred to snakes in order to convey the idea of a stealthy movement. Since creeping implies not being seen and distinguishes animal motion, it is used to indicate the chaotic dynamism of the unconscious, which constantly eludes the grasp of consciousness, and is applied to birds because the insight they spontaneously turn into singing belongs to the realm of unconscious imagination. In a certain sense, serpents and birds may be said to share the same starting point.

question of how to turn the vision into words in a Romantic way, it is nonetheless Keats's first acknowledgement – as well as representation – that a problem of verbalisation actually exists. If he had wanted to convey the ease and spontaneity of the transformation of the contents of imagination into poetry, he would have resorted to the image of the bird rather than to the pained, suffocating serpent.

The interpretation of the bird within this metapoetic frame of reference is confirmed by the interesting passage in the verse letter to Reynolds that has already been analysed as one of the first instances where Keats questions the power of imagination. Here, the imaginative ability of human beings to see things that are not present is said to prevent the enjoyment of the present moment in the form of spoiling "the singing of the nightingale" ("To J. H. Reynolds, Esq." 85). Yet, these lines have also been interpreted as a representation of the impasse in which imagination can find itself due to the necessity to submit its insights to the convergent laws of language in spite of their divergent nature. As a result, the singing of the nightingale is spoiled also because it symbolises an unmediated spontaneity of communication that the seeming incompatibility between vision – which follows the symmetrical law of "heaven" (82) – and its necessary poetic verbalisation – which responds to the asymmetrical law of "earth" (82) – makes impossible. However, the role of bird symbolism in Keats's poetry would require a more in-depth analysis than I can here afford without straying too much from my main topic, and, therefore, may be adequately dealt with in a general study on Keats's animal imagery.

4.3 Hyperion

Keats undertook the composition of *Hyperion* in autumn 1818 and abandoned it in April 1819, so that Book 1 probably dates back to the last few months of 1818. Between *Endymion* and *Hyperion* snakes are present only in *Isabella*, another narrative poem, but not very interestingly, as already pointed out. Although *Hyperion* presents a lesser concentration of serpent imagery (6.1 %) than Book 3 of *Endymion* (12.1 %) or *Lamia* (45.5 %) – the snakes are, indeed, two and I will focus only on the most meaningful –, it constitutes a fundamental turning point in Keats's serpent symbolism. In Book 1, Keats describes Hyperion, who is the only Titan not to have fallen yet, while he is walking through his palace and is beholding ghastly omens of doom for the first time. He is distraught by the contemplation of "these horrors new" (*Hyperion* I 233) even in his "centre of repose" (243), and wonders whether he is destined to share the same fate as Saturn's, when a mist starts to arise amid the phantoms.

> At this, through all his bulk an agony
> Crept gradual, from the feet unto the crown,
> Like a lithe serpent vast and muscular
> Making slow way, with head and neck convulsed
> From over-strainèd might [...] (259-263)

Suddenly released, Hyperion flees away, but he is soon forced to acknowledge his decrease in power, since he cannot command the dawn anymore. As far as the simile of the snake is concerned, it presents some very interesting characteristics, which have been proven to be of paramount importance in Keats's development of this symbol. First of all, the serpent is depicted in motion. It creeps through Hyperion's whole body in a gradual and slow way, as if to reach every limb thanks to its developed muscular system. 'Serpent' is accompanied by three adjectives that are all focused on its corporeality and on its flexibility, size, and muscularity, respectively. It belongs to the dimension of the dynamic, animal body, that is, to the instinctual, preverbal unconscious. It is, however, noteworthy that the three adjectives are placed in different positions, as one precedes the verb, while the other two follow it. Thus, "lithe" (261) turns out to be isolated and consequently emphasised, which is confirmed on a metrical level, since it bears the first beat of the line due to a rising inversion. The division of the adjectives in two groups derives from the fact that, just as "vast" and "muscular" describe the bulk of the serpent, so "lithe" focuses on its extraordinary capacity of movement. A dynamic attribute is followed by static ones, but it also coincides with a metrical device that, after an initial acceleration, slows down the rhythm and almost stops the flow of the line in the two consecutive beats[192] before returning to a flat regular path. A sudden peak of semantic and metrical dynamism ends, thus, in a static suspension. The same alternation – or even coexistence – of motion and stasis is found in the following line, which presents the same semantical division between a first part dominated by an image of dynamism (263: "Making slow way") and a second one marked by stillness ("with head and neck convulsed"). What is more, due to another rising inversion at the beginning of the line, "slow way" presents two consecutive beats, so that the movement of the serpent is slowed down on a metrical level too, and almost blocked.

It is thus evident that the passage does not convey the sense of anarchic movement that was found in the episode of Circe. As a matter of fact, some restraint already emerges from the phrase "Crept gradual" (260), where the

---

192 Attridge describes the rhythmic experience of the rising inversion in the following terms: "Two unstressed syllables (usually of equal lightness) lead into a stressed beat and then another, equally strong or even stronger, stressed beat. The alternating rhythm is challenged and then restored, the movement is speeded up and then slowed down. The words containing the stressed beats usually stand out as emphatic" (121).

adjective substitutes the adverb[193]. As verbs express actions and are more dynamic than nouns by definition, so are adverbs, which modify the former, more dynamic than adjectives, which modify the latter. Therefore, the movement that is conveyed through the verb seems to be somewhat constrained by the adjective. The morphological level is paralleled by the metrical one, and the rhythm is extremely slowed down in "gradual" by the presence of two beats in the same word. A similar succession is repeated when it comes to the other verb of movement. In fact, the dynamic present participle "Making" (262) is followed by two static past participles, "convulsed" (262) and "over-strainèd" (263), which both convey the contraction affecting the serpent's head and neck. In conclusion, the whole passage is dominated by the tension between inexorable movement and hindrance, which makes the snake's progression across Hyperion's body painful and a perfect simile for agony.

The fact that the convulsion is concentrated in the neck develops the loose association between the serpent and stifling that was present in *Endymion* and has important metapoetic implications, as already pointed out. The contraction of the neck implies the obstruction of the vocal tract, thus preventing vocal emission, which is confirmed on a phonosymbolic level. There is again a constant tension between block and release, which is rendered through a succession, respectively, of plosives, whose manner of articulation implies an obstruction of the vocal tract, and continuous sounds, such as liquids, especially in clusters. This dynamics is particularly evident in some of the most semantically as well as metrically relevant words of the passage, such as the stressed "bulk" (259), where the initial plosive is followed by two continuous sounds – a vowel and then a liquid –, as if to convey a regained free flowing of sound, but the [l] is in cluster with [k]. The word ends, thus, with a total obstruction, which is emphasised by the fact that three voiced phonemes precede a final voiceless one[194]. A similar phonetic pattern is found in the phrase that describes the strenuous movement of the serpent through Hyperion's body, i.e. "Crept gradual" (260). "Crept" begins and ends with a consonantal cluster: the former is a releasing one, since the voiceless plosive [k] is followed by the voiced liquid [r], whereas the latter represents a total obstruction, as it consists in two consecutive voiceless plosives. The dynamics is quite recurrent in the whole passage, and suggests the idea of a constrained energy that is momentarily released only to be restrained again – a sequence that is repeated throughout the snake's progression in Hyperion's bulk. After the hindering effect of "crept", in fact, "gradual" seems to present a

---

193 Bate accounts for the use of the adjective simply by ascribing it to Milton's stylistic influence (69), which is true, but can be also further explained.
194 Voiceless plosives are articulated without a vibration of the vocal cords, thus they are perceived as more blocking than voiced ones.

partial unblocking of the flow. The voiced velar plosive at the beginning turns into a voiced rhotic, and the word ends with the voiced alveolar lateral approximant. Moreover, both syllables are metrically stressed.

The passage, however, ends with a strong image of suffocation, i.e. "neck convulsed / From over-strainèd might" (262–263), where a sense of restraint is conveyed not only on a semantic level but also on a phonosymbolic one. The obstructing effect of the [k] at the end of a stressed syllable in "neck" is intensified by the fact that the following word begins with the same phoneme. What is more, "convulsed" ends with a cluster of three consonants that is emphasised by another metrical beat, and goes from the voiced continuous lateral [l] to the voiceless plosive [t] through the mediation of the voiceless continuous fricative [s], so that the direction is clearly towards a gradual but complete block, which is further highlighted precisely by its own gradualness. It has already been said that the cluster [st] is among the highest degrees of obstruction; indeed, it is found in the central stressed syllable of "over-strainèd", where it is followed by the voiced, continuous [r], as if to suggest a release that is denied by the final [d]. This last plosive is actually emphasised by the fact that, in this case, the preceding vowel needs to be pronounced. The concentration of blocking clusters in "convulsed" and "over-strainèd" is meaningful, since they are the two terms that most evidently semanticise constriction, the former by pointing at the contraction of the neck, whereas the latter by indicating the effect of an excessive effort.

If it is true that release and restraint are kept in tension on different levels of the text throughout this passage, it is also evident from what has been said so far that the latter seems, in the end, to prevail, so that the appearance of the serpent coincides with some hindrance, which is rather opposite to the resolving power of the serpentine flame in *Endymion*. This interpretation is confirmed by the phonosymbolism that accompanies the mention of the snake. "Like a lithe serpent vast" (261) begins with two words that have a very similar phonetic structure, as, in both cases, the [l] is followed by the diphthong [aɪ] and, then, by another consonant. "Like", however, ends with the blocking [k], whose obstructing effect is emphasised by the extended vocal emission of the preceding diphthong, as seen in the passage from *Endymion*. Conversely, "lithe", which has been pointed out to be more significant on a metric and syntactic level, substitutes the voiceless velar plosive with a voiced dental fricative, which interrupts the isotopy of blocked articulation in favour of a flowing that still suggests a constriction, since fricatives are articulated by forcing the air through a narrowed passage. Every passage in these lines is painful and requires some effort. The [ð] turns, then, into the voiceless sibilant at the beginning of snake, but the obstruction returns in the final [t] of the word, and is intensified in the following "vast", as it ends with the most blocking cluster [st], which is further intensified by the preceding long vowel [ɑː], in accordance with the dominating pattern of momentary release and prevailing constraint.

After pointing out the pervasiveness of elements signifying hindrance and strain in association with the appearance of the snake, the nature of this hindrance should now be examined. As a matter of fact, the difficulty that Hyperion is facing is explicitly asserted a few lines before, when he "spake, and ceased, the while a heavier threat / Held struggle with his throat but came not forth" (251–252). Hyperion would add something to his speech, but he is impeded, as the words do not come out of his throat. On a formal level, there are again elements that convey the tension of a restrained energy. The syntax is fragmented at the beginning of line 251, as if to represent with its strong pauses Hyperion's abrupt difficulty of speech, but it then resumes its flowing even beyond the boundaries of the lines through an enjambment. As far as the phonosymbolic level is concerned, there is a recurring sequence of fricatives followed by diphthongs or long vowels that intensify the blocking effect of the final voiceless plosive and are contained in metrically stressed syllables: "spake"[195], "ceased", "threat" (251) and "throat"[196] (252).

The convulsion of the snake's neck suggests the same idea of impeded speech, since the contraction of the throat implies suffocation and prevents vocal emission, which corresponds to verbal expression, that is, on a metapoetic level, communication through poetry. The concentration of blocking phonemes and clusters that has been pointed out conveys precisely the difficulty of articulation, which is further suggested through the high number of voiceless velar plosives[197]. The consonant [k] is, indeed, particularly suited to convey the sense of blocked phonation. Being a voiceless plosive, it is produced through an obstruction of the vocal tract and without letting the air pass across the vocal cords, but its velar articulation means that it is produced nearer to the throat, thus resembling more the sound of a convulsed one even on an onomatopoetic level. It is noteworthy to take into account this aspect also because voiceless velar plosives are much fewer in the passage of *Endymion* that has been analysed, and, what is more, they appear together with the snake but not with the mention of stifling, which is a further proof that the isotopy of suffocation as difficulty of verbal expression in association with the serpent is not fully developed yet.

According to the paradigm of interpretation that has been applied so far, the sudden apparition of the snake[198] can be identified again with the emergence of

---

195 In this case, the initial sibilant is included in the blocking cluster [sp].
196 The word "throat" belongs to the phrase "struggle with his throat" (252), so that the final plosive parallels the initial cluster [st] and stops the flow released by the consecutive [r].
197 See "bulk" (259), "Crept", "crown" (260), "Like", "muscular" (261), "Making", "neck", "convulsed" (262).
198 It comes as unexpectedly as the "mist" (258), to which, in fact, the serpent is isomorphic.

the imaginative insight to consciousness. The serpent is depicted with a strong focus on his corporeality, so that it is ascribable to the preverbal, preconceptual dimension of the unconscious. The moment it appears, it produces an intense emotive impact on Hyperion and, on the metapoetic level, on the consciousness of the poet, as is proven by the corresponding distortion of the metre. The mention of the snake, in fact, coincides with two rising inversions at the beginning of lines 261 and 262 in an otherwise metrically regular passage. This emotive impact generates a tension between the vision and the necessity to communicate it by means of language, a tension that is painful and problematic, as the two dimensions respond to the opposite laws of the symmetrical and asymmetrical mode, respectively. It should be here remembered that the need to turn the insight into words is not implied by the normal functioning of the former, but depends on the assumption of the role of poet, since poets alone can and must tell their vision, as Keats asserts in the opening lines of *The Fall of Hyperion*[199]. The poet's task is to bridge the gap between divergent vision and convergent language. The generation of a tension between the two is made clear in the passage from *Hyperion*, as the movement of the serpent faces elements of restraint that work on different levels of the text and focus mainly on blocked phonation. However, the motion of the snake is never entirely stopped, so that from this unresolved tension a 'living symbol' is created. All this constrained energy is finally "Released" (263) through the sudden flee of Hyperion, which is marked by a medial full-stop after the accented syllable of "might" (263). This masculine kind of caesura slows down the rhythm of the line, by shifting the pause from after the fourth syllable to after the sixth one, and conveys a more solemn, heavy pace[200]. The coincidence of a syntactic and metrical pause renders it incredibly strong. It breaks the line in order to represent, at the same time, the climax of tension and its unexpected release.

As said when dealing with *Endymion*, the problem of poetic verbalisation is not limited to the different functioning of language compared to the contents of imagination, although this opposition can be considered as the basis of the whole issue. By adding the adjective 'poetic' to 'verbalisation', the focus is on the way the vision is conveyed not only through words, but specifically through poetry, so that some issues of poetics are concerned, such as that of the composition of a long narrative poem in *Endymion*. Therefore, I will now analyse the reason why the serpent as powerful image of pain and suffocation is found precisely in *Hyperion* after some suggestions in Book 3 of *Endymion*. *Hyperion*

---

199 See line 8: "For Poesy alone can tell her dream".
200 Bate points out that "the only major English pentameter writer who shows consistent preference for it [the masculine caesura after a stressed syllable] is Milton, who sought a majestic and dignified line" (209), so that this metrical device has to be ascribed to Milton's stylistic influence upon *Hyperion*.

was the first narrative poem of a considerable length that Keats attempted after the composition of *Endymion*. When Ridley wonders what has happened to account for the stylistic difference between the two poems, he does not hesitate to assert that "Milton has happened" (67). The influence of Milton on *Hyperion* is widely acknowledged by critics[201] as well as by Keats himself, and is usually considered to be more pervasive in Book 1, where the passage of the serpent comes from. Just as Milton was held as a model on a stylistic and prosodic level, he also became one of Keats's major sources as far as serpent imagery is concerned. I have already pointed out how the snake in Book 1 of *Hyperion* was probably inspired by a passage from *Paradise Lost*, which stroke him with the sense of suffocation it conveys, so that he was brought to ascribe a stifled throat directly to a serpent. From this moment on, Milton's depictions of snakes continued to inspire Keats, as is proven by their significant echoes in *Lamia*.

Keats resorted to Milton's stylistic model, which is rather unusual for a Romantic poet, in order to treat his subject "in a more naked and grecian Manner" and in an "undeviating" (*Letters*, vol. 1, 207) way that departs from the narrative and actantial wanderings of *Endymion*. Just as, through the latter, Keats had attempted to follow the divergent free flowing of imagination, he now aimed at a greater control on his matter and at a new structural coherence. According to Bate, the entire stylistic development of *Hyperion* is "in the direction of intensity and restraint" (91). Bate's use of the term 'restraint' is rather interesting, as it has been applied to the impeded movement of the serpent in the passage that has just been analysed. Overall, Keats endeavoured to write with more discipline than he had done before, or with more "judgement" (*Letters*, vol. 1, 374), as he himself wrote in the letter dated on 8 October 1818, the same month in which he started composing *Hyperion*. Discipline, judgement, and control, however, are all terms that belong to the convergent part of the creative process and are nearer to the Augustan conception of creativity[202] than to the Romantic one, which favours, instead, its divergent aspects. In light of this, the tension that constitutes the symbol of the serpent in *Hyperion* can be interpreted as the opposition between the unconscious, symmetrical nature of the insight and the asymmetrical constraints that are imposed upon it not simply by language, but by a way of composing which is dominated by conscious, rational effort.

Yet the outcome does not seem to be presented as really successful, as the sense of suffocation overwhelms Hyperion who flees away. He does not manage to give voice to the "heavier threat" (*Hyperion* I 251) he sensed, but rather sees it

---

201 See, at least, Ridley 67–95 and Bate 66–91.
202 Furthermore, in *Hyperion*, Bate identifies a tendency that runs parallel to the Miltonic influence and corresponds to "a general inclination throughout Keats's entire technical development to return gradually, in a degree surpassing most of his contemporaries, to the skeletal integrity of the Augustan line" (86).

confirmed by his diminished powers, so that his release is only partial. That the dysphoric dimension of painful constriction dominates the scene is echoed on the metapoetic level, since the limitations imposed by the Miltonic model and these new creative principles soon became too limiting to Keats who abandoned the composition of the poem. On 21 September 1819, Keats expressed his changed opinion on Milton in two letters, where he compared him with Chatterton in favour of the latter. He wrote to George and Georgiana: "Miltonic verse cannot be written but it [*for* in] the vein of art – I wish to devote myself to another sensation" (*Letters*, vol. 2, 212), but he confirmed his newly developed aversion to Milton in stronger terms: "Life to him would be death to me" (*ibidem*). Moreover, in the letter to Reynolds he directly linked the refusal of Milton with his decision to abandon *Hyperion*, which actually dates back to April of the same year: "I have given up Hyperion – there were too many Miltonic inversions in it – Miltonic verse cannot be written but in an artful, or, rather, artist's humour. I wish to give myself to other sensations" (*Letters*, vol. 2, 167). Keats identifies the excess of metrical inversions as the reason why he could not finish the poem, but the problem is actually more general, as is proven by his insistence on the term 'art' to describe the artificiality of Milton's style. In the same letter to Reynolds, he goes on to write: "It may be interesting to you to pick out some line from Hyperion, and put a mark x to the false beauty proceeding from art, and one || to the true voice of feeling. Upon my soul 'twas imagination – I cannot make the distinction – Every now and then there is a Miltonic intonation – But I cannot make the division properly" (*ibidem*). Keats here returns to the opposition between a rationalist way of composing, which produces false beauty through conscious craftsmanship and imitation, and the Romantic one, which aims at an authentic expression of the poet's feelings.

After praising the importance of judgement and discipline, as well as trying to apply them in *Hyperion*, Keats returned to assert a faith in the Romantic principles, and it is not by chance that the interruption of the composition of *Hyperion* coincides with the writing of the famous lyric odes, which present a purely Romantic inspiration. It is also noteworthy that Keats turned from Milton, who was rejected because of his disciplined, artificial style, but also because his too strong influence prevented Keats from expressing his authentic voice, to Chatterton, who was considered as the prototype of the Romantic genius and to whom he had dedicated *Endymion*. In addition, a return to the Romantic conception of creativity meant a reaffirmation of imagination as chief faculty of poetic composition; indeed, in the letter to George and Georgiana, Keats defined his art in the following terms: "I describe what I imagine" (*Letters*, vol. 2, 200). In the letter to Reynolds, however, imagination is more ambiguous, as Keats confessed that he could not distinguish between the moments of Miltonic, rationalist artificiality and those of Romantic authenticity, because they all seemed to originate from imagination. Keats could not return to an unproblematic faith in imagination after confronting the dangers of its unbound use[203] and the resulting necessity of its restraint that led to the stylistic revolution of *Hyperion*. At the same time, while writing *Hyperion*, he also experienced the risks the limitation of the divergent, imaginative faculty can involve. The serpent symbolises this crucial moment, when the convergent restraints imposed on the imaginative insight in order to communicate it are about to become too suffocating.

This overview of Keats's poetic ideas during the composition of *Hyperion* and immediately after has been useful to better understand the specific tension that generates the 'living symbol' in *Hyperion*. The correspondence between the sense of restraint in the snake's depiction and the limiting aspects of the Miltonic model is further justified by the fact that Milton, as already seen, is Keats's major source as far as the elements of contortion and suffocation in serpent imagery are concerned. However, even the letters where Keats rejected Milton and seemed to return to a purely Romantic conception of creativity are not an arrival point. In accordance with the properties of living symbols, the tension between spontaneous, unbound imagination and the need for some restraint was never resolved[204]. After the composition of the odes, in fact, Keats reverted to some stylistic tendencies of *Hyperion* and completely carried them out in *Lamia*. A perfect example of this process is the fact that inversions, to whom he had ascribed his decision to interrupt *Hyperion*, are even more frequent in *Lamia*[205].

4.4 *Lamia*

Unsurprisingly, *Lamia* constitutes the culminating moment of serpent symbolism in Keats's entire poetic production, as it revolves around the ambiguous figure of a serpent-woman and includes almost half of all the mentions of snakes. Lamia is, indeed, a supernatural creature that is endowed with a double nature: she is both a serpent and a woman, never entirely the former or the latter, but always something in between, even though she turns from being mainly a snake to being mainly a woman during the narration. This twofoldness of her nature

---

203 See the verse letter to Reynolds (25 March 1818), "On Visiting the Tomb of Burns" (1 July 1818) and *Letters* 93 (10 June 1818), all dating back to the period between the composition of *Endymion* and that of *Hyperion*.

204 For instance, Keats returned to the need to curb imagination with judgement in April 1819 (*Letters*, vol. 2, 97), during the period of the composition of the odes, which is usually considered as his most Romantic one.

205 See the table in Seright 53, where she lists the average number of inversions of word order per line in Keats's most important poems and shows that they are more numerous in Book 1 of *Lamia* (0.164) than in Book 1 of *Hyperion* (0.160).

needs to be always borne in mind when analysing the poem and its main character. Lamia first appears to Hermes as "a palpitating snake, / Bright, and cirque-couchant in a dusky brake" (*Lamia* I 45–46), where each adjective points out one of the important characteristics that have been identified while dealing with the physical description of serpents.

'Palpitating' suggests the idea of somewhat irregularly repeated movement, which is phonosymbolically conveyed through the repetition of plosives. The word 'palpitating' itself presents a succession of two voiceless bilabial stops followed by two voiceless alveolar stops. Patterns of carefully repeating sounds, as will be seen, are used to represent the action of hypnotism too, which often induces trance by repeating series of musical sounds. It is not the case of 'palpitating', since the repeated phonemes are plosives and voiceless ones, while musicality distinguishes continuous, voiced phonemes – and, in particular, periodic ones – at the highest degree[206], so that the mesmeric effect is stronger when the latter are present. It is, therefore, only partially achieved in the following line, where the voiced cluster [br] is repeated in chiasmus with [k][207]. Moreover, 'bright' itself refers to the "dazzling" (47) – and thus hypnotic – appearance of the serpent. 'Cirque-couchant', instead, is a neologism to indicate its being coiled, which will be specifically defined as a twisted shape through the adjective "gordian" (47). The same adjective was used to describe a snake in the analysed passage in Book 3 of *Endymion*, with whom these lines from *Lamia* share more than one element. In both cases, in fact, the intricacy of the serpent is paralleled by that of the brake[208] where it is found. In addition, "brake" is here accompanied by "dusky", which recreates the same dim setting as the forest on Circe's island, as darkness is a fundamental attribute in the representation of the unconscious. Lamia's belonging to the dimension of the unconscious is further stressed by her supernatural nature. She comes from the Other World, which is presented in the initial frame of the poem as the extrahuman dwelling of gods, such as Hermes, and nymphs.

Lamia's description, which is also Keats's longest description of a serpent-like creature, continues in the following way:

She was a gordian shape of dazzling hue,
Vermilion-spotted, golden, green and blue;
Striped like a zebra, freckled like a pard,
Eyed like a peacock, and all crimson barred;

---

206 Tsur ascribes musicality to periodic sounds, i. e. vowels, semivowels, liquids and nasals, and to continuous ones (66). When dealing with the musical perception of periodic sounds due to their being experienced as "smoothly flowing" (44), he also mentions Snyder's identification of periodic phonemes with hypnotic sounds (45–47).
207 "Bright, and cirque-couchant in a dusky brake" (*Lamia* I 46).
208 See the "thorny brake" in *Endymion* III 493.

> And full of silver moons, that, as she breathed,
> Dissolved, or brighter shone, or interwreathed
> Their lustres with the gloomier tapestries –
> So rainbow-sided, touched with miseries,
> She seemed, at once, some penanced lady elf,
> Some demon's mistress, or the demon's self. (47-56)

The first five lines present a high concentration of noun modifiers according to the tendency towards their clustering that Seright identifies in Keats's later poetry[209]. All the eleven noun modifiers – be they adjectives or propositional phrases – are referred to "shape" (*Lamia* I 47), which is a neutral noun, since it does not convey any particular information about the snake. "It is the modifiers", as Seright says, "which bring the noun 'shape' into specific perspective" (11). It follows that, in opposition to what is traditionally thought, noun modifiers become the most important part of speech, a characteristic that Seright identifies as the main constant of Keats's style and that leads to the predominance of a descriptive as well as presentative mode of discourse (2-4).

These general considerations take on specific meaning when applied to the passage from *Lamia*. If a description becomes more precise in direct proportion to the number of attributes added, they here raise to almost an excessive concentration without conveying any true idea of precision. Lamia's skin, in fact, seems to possess so many colours and patterns that it needs to be compared to that of other animals. Similes, however, are not a way of defining something accurately, but rather of getting closer to it through something that is similar only indirectly. Similes do not tell what things are, but what they look like. Lamia is said to resemble a zebra, a leopard, and a peacock, but she still remains undefinable. If it is true that definitions usually revolve around nouns, Lamia is referred to simply as a "shape" (147), a term which is so general that, as already said, it turns out to be devoid of actual information. Thus, the extreme concentration of noun modifiers around a single neutral noun, as well as the recourse to similes, identify Lamia's description as an attempt to define as precisely as possible what eludes definition. It is an asymptotic approximation to something whose inexhaustible richness cannot be entirely grasped through language, which, according to what has been considered so far, can be easily applied to the products of imagination, so that an association between the serpent and the imaginative insight is established again. Moreover, the character-

---

[209] See Seright 63-65. She draws from *Lamia* also other examples of heavy noun modification, most of which are referred either to Lamia (I 45-46, 150-151, II 71), to her magically adorned palace (II 143-144), or to Apollonius's serpent-like stare (II 300-301). This means that most of them are somehow related to a serpent.

istics that Lamia shares with Endymion's snake further point in this same direction.

Lamia is approached by listing what she *seems* in lines 55–56 too, where she is said to resemble simultaneously a penanced fairy and the demon, with a shift from her physical appearance to her axiological value. This means that she is both someone who is afflicted by sorrow and someone who makes others suffer, and, as a matter of fact, the doubt whether Lamia is the victim or the villain of the story runs through the whole poem. The coexistence of opposite axiological connotations is one of the main requisites of a 'living symbol', but it also links Lamia to symmetrical logic, which does not respect the Aristotelian principle of non-contradiction[210], thus allowing her to have contradictory properties at the same time[211]. As already said, it is symmetrical logic that dominates unconscious imagination. Lamia's belonging to the realm of the latter is further suggested by her visionary powers, which manifest themselves mainly through dreams: "first 'tis fit to tell how she could muse / And dream, when in the serpent prison-house, / Of all she list, strange or magnificent" (I 202–204). The serpent's body is here presented as a form of confinement which yet comprehends the unbound capability of movement of Lamia's spirit (205: "ever, where she willed, her spirit went"). 'Dreaming' is a term that Keats often uses in order to indicate the activity of imagination[212], and, what is more, Lamia's dreams are always Adam's dreams: she awakes and finds them true. This is particularly evident as far as her meeting with Hermes is concerned. Indeed, she addresses him by saying: "I had a splendid dream of thee last night" (I 69), and concludes in the following way: "I dreamt I saw thee [...] and here thou art!" (76, 79), exactly like Eve is in front of Adam when he wakes from his dream.

As the serpent's body is compared to a prison, it is noteworthy that, in Lamia's description, adjectives with -ed ending replace those with -ing ending. The former, in fact, are static, or rather convey the idea of "an energy momentarily caught at rest and condensed and *imprisoned* [italics added] within an otherwise static image" (Bate 96)[213], whereas the latter are purely dynamic. At the beginning, Lamia is said to be "palpitating" (*Lamia* I 45), a present participle

---

210 On the lack of mutual contradiction in the symmetrical mode, see Matte Blanco 40, 43–45.
211 In addition, Stewart interestingly points out that "The disjunctive series places the inclusive 'at once' at logical odds with the contrastive 'or', as if to remind us of the failure of consecutive or categorical reasoning in the face of such wonder" (12).
212 One example out of many is found in the incipit of *The Fall of Hyperion*, which was begun in July 1819, that is, in the same period as *Lamia*'s composition.
213 Bate makes this remark regarding *Hyperion*, whereas he considers the adjectives with -ed ending in *Lamia* to be more conventional (148). It will be seen, instead, that they correspond to an important aspect of the serpent's characterisation.

that expresses some kind of movement also semantically, and "dazzling" (47)[214], but then past participles as adjectives prevail, such as "vermilion-spotted" (48), "Striped", "freckled" (49), "[e]yed", "barred" (50), "rainbow-sided", "touched" (54), "penanced" (55). The opposition between these two patterns creates a tension, as, despite the natural capability of movement of the snake, Lamia experiences her current state as the most static, that is, as death. Not only is the serpent's body a prison, but it is also a "wreathèd tomb" (38), where there are again an adjective with -ed ending and the element of intricacy, which also marks the following description (see, for instance, "interwreathed" in line 52). The twisted shape stands for something that is not linear as well as for a path that is not effortless to tread. The serpent is again associated with some kind of hindrance, and Lamia finds herself in an impasse. She is trapped in her serpentine condition, and the only way to free herself is turning into a woman, into a "sweet body fit for life" (49). Lastly, it is not by chance that an adjective with -ing ending reappears in the passage when Lamia's human voice is concerned (64–65: "Her throat was serpent, but the words she spake / Came, as through bubbling honey, for love's sake").

As already seen, Lamia differs from all other snakes because she is endowed with the faculty of speech and, what is more, with a musical, hypnotic voice[215]. The mesmeric powers of her words are made evident by Hermes's reaction to them: the god of movement is immobilised "Like a stooped falcon" (67). The effect of sudden paralysis is stressed by the metrical rising inversion at the beginning of line 67, where two offbeats are followed by two consecutive beats, so that the rhythm is first accelerated only to be strongly slowed down when it comes to the still falcon. As already hinted at, the magic power of Lamia's voice is phonosymbolically conveyed through carefully organised patterns of repeating phonemes. A meaningful example is the spell thanks to which she allows Hermes to see the nymph: "Stoop, Hermes, let me breathe upon thy brow, / And thou shalt see thy sweet nymph even now" (121–122). The first line presents a consonantal chiasmus between [br] and [ð][216], while the second a vocalic one between [aʊ] and [iː][217] as well as a consonantal parallelism that involves [ð], [s] and [n][218]. The effect of the spell is hypnotic, as confirmed by the monotony of

---

214 Adjectives in–ing are found in the immediately preceding lines too, even if not directly referred to Lamia: "soft-brushing" (43) and "full-flowering" (44).
215 The fact that Lamia seduces Lycius through her mesmeric singing makes her resemble Circe and, indeed, her head is said to be "Circean" (I 115).
216 The elements of the consonantal chiasmus are underlined: "breathe upon thy brow" (121).
217 The elements of the vocalic chiasmus are underlined: "thou shalt see thy sweet nymph even now" (122).
218 The elements of the consonantal parallelism are underlined: "thou shalt see thy sweet nymph even now" (122).

the metre, with the exception of the first two consecutive beats in "Stoop, Hermes" (121), which recall the image of the stooped falcon in line 67 and of an immobilised, "hovering" (129) Hermes. However, not all the phonemes that are involved in these lines are musical as required by hypnotism. Some of them are fricatives and, precisely, fricatives with a sibilant effect, which have often been ascribed to animal noise and onomatopoetically represent Lamia's "swift-lisping" (116) pronunciation. Apart from suggesting a certain difficulty in articulation and the unpleasantness of the result, her defective pronunciation of the [s] draws the attention on this phoneme and is reminiscent of the hiss of a serpent.

Sibilants become dominant every time Lamia's nature is dealt with both before[219] and after her transformation into a woman[220]. The swift-lisping nature of Lamia's voice seems to contradict its hypnotic musicality, but the coexistence of these two qualities seems rather to confirm Lamia's fundamental twofoldness on the vocal level, which is the one most directly linked with the production of poetry and, thus, extremely important for the present analysis. On one hand, there are vowels, liquids and nasals, which are perceived as melodious sounds thanks to their periodic nature, and belong to the euphoric realm of human voice. On the other, there are fricatives, especially sibilants, which are aperiodic, often voiceless and nearer to the dysphoric dimension of animal noise. Lamia takes part in the former as a woman and in the latter as a serpent. What is noteworthy is that these two qualities of Lamia's voice always coexist – though to different extents – and the first words she says after her metamorphosis serve as an example: "Lycius! Gentle Lycius!" (168). The insistence on the voiced alveolar lateral approximant conveys the sense of human musicality, but this music remains serpentine due to the persistence of voiceless sibilants. The same pattern is found when describing Lamia's unearthly song, whose mesmeric potential is rendered through parallel successions of [s] and [l] at the beginning of words: "A song of love, too sweet for earthly lyres" (299)[221].

---

219 See, for instance, the concentration of sibilants in the following lines from the passage that has already been analysed: "And full of silver moons, that, as she breathed, / Dissolved, or brighter shone, or interwreathed / Their lustres with the gloomier tapestries – / So rainbow-sided, touched with miseries, / She seemed, at once, some penanced lady elf, / Some demon's mistress, or the demon's self" (51–56).
220 Sibilants become again dominant when Lamia speaks of her essence: "What taste of purer air hast thou to soothe / My essence? What serener palaces, / Where I may all my many senses please, / And by mysterious sleights a hundred thirsts appease?" (I 282–285). These lines also present an iteration of [m] at the beginning of words, as the voiced bilabial nasal is a musical, tender phoneme that often marks the representation of pleasure. According to Tsur, the softness of the nasals – as for the liquids – depends on their being the least coded consonants as well as continuous and periodical (see Tsur, chapter 1).
221 A similar insistence on [l] and [s] in initial stressed syllables is found in the immediately preceding lines: "He, sick to lose / The amorous promise of her lone complain, / Swooned, murmuring of love, and pale with pain. / The cruel lady, without any show / Of sorrow [...]

The insuppressible bipolarity of Lamia's voice and nature, however, does not cancel the fundamental value of her metamorphosis from serpent into woman, which I will now focus on. The role of heat in the passage from cold-blooded creature to warm-blooded one has already been stressed, yet the dominating isotopy is undoubtedly that of pain. During Lamia's transformation, her eyes are "in torture fixed and anguished drear" (150) and flash phosphor "without one cooling tear" (152), while she "writhe[s] about, convulsed in scarlet pain" (154). Lamia's pain is red because it is originated by an attempt to approach the world of humans. Just as blue is the coldest colour, as said when dealing with the flame in *Endymion*, and thus conveys the greatest sense of distance, so red seems to approach the spectator due to its warm nature[222]. Lamia is suffering because she is trying to come closer to the human world, i.e. our world, and to human emotionality from her former condition of serpent, that is, from what is the remotest from man. The ontological gap between extrahuman[223] and human is wide, so that overcoming it cannot but be painful. Her suffering takes the form of convulsions, which, as pointed out, are usually paralleled by corresponding contractions of the vocal tract. Although in this case they are not semantically present in the passage, they are still suggested through the concentration of voiceless plosives, in particular velar ones[224], which are the most suited phonemes to convey the idea of suffocation as well as blocked phonation. As usual, clusters that are composed of continuous phonemes followed by a plosive represent total obstruction, whereas the contrary combination stands for final partial release. Among the latter, it is noteworthy the recourse to a succession of the phonemes [k] and [l] until they form the cluster [kl][225], which is not present in *Endymion* or *Hyperion* and combines the most choking plosive with the musical liquid, which will characterize Lamia's "new voice luting soft" (167).

Lamia's whole transformation is here exemplified. The passage from the

    she began to sing / Happy in beauty, life, and love, and everything" (287-298). The two phonemes even come together in "slow" (293), which bears a metrical beat, and reappear when Lamia's singing is mentioned again: "To see her still, and singing so sweet lays; / Then from amaze into delight he fell / To hear her whisper woman's lore so well" (323-325).
222 According to Kandinsky, red possesses an "unbound warmth" (40) and, therefore, like all warm colours, it is perceived as if it approached the viewer (80).
223 Lamia shares characteristics of both the subhuman and the superhuman, since she is both an animal and a fairy.
224 Voiceless plosives are underlined in the following lines: "Flashed phosphor and sharp sparks, without one cooling tear. / The colours all inflamed throughout her train, / She writhed about, convulsed with scarlet pain. / A deep volcanian yellow took the place / Of all her milder-moonèd body's grace; / And, as the lava vanishes the mead, / Spoilt all her silver mail, and golden brede; / Made gloom of all her frecklings, streaks and bars, / Eclipsed her crescents, and licked up her stars" (152-160).
225 This device is called diminution (Tsur 40). See the passage from "cooling" (152) and "colours" (153) to "frecklings" (159) and "eclipsed" (160).

convulsed articulation of plosives to a new musicality can be interpreted as the passage from animal noise to human singing, that is, from serpent to woman, but also from the inarticulate to the articulate, from the nonverbal to the verbal. On a metapoetic level, in fact, obstructed phonation suggests a difficulty in producing language which, unsurprisingly, corresponds to Lamia's transformation from snake to woman. If it is true that Lamia shares some important qualities with the imaginative insight – as, in general, Keatsian serpents do –, her passage from the supernatural Other World to the world of men symbolises the act of verbalisation through which the insight that is produced by the unconscious imagination is transformed into poetry and communicated, as confirmed by the fact that the first element which appears after Lamia's metamorphosis is her musical voice. Hence, also her suffering, as well as Keats's recurrent association of serpents with pain, acquire new specific meaning. Just as her pain originates from her necessity to overcome the ontological gap between extrahuman and human, so this same gap metapoetically corresponds to the one between the symmetrical functioning of imagination and the asymmetrical laws of language, which is also conveyed by the impossibility to define Lamia through the limitations of convergent language in her first description. Ultimately, Lamia's vanishing from her supernatural world of nymphs and gods (165–166) and her following reappearance in the world of men depict the poet's act of bringing his inner vision to its outer realisation in poetry.

Lamia experiences her snake's body as a prison because she longs to be turned into a woman. Just as the snake is associated with the emergence of the insight to consciousness through its sudden manifestation – and Lamia herself appears to Lycius unexpectedly (35) –, the person who has assumed the role of the poet feels the urge to communicate this insight. Until he manages, he finds himself in a creative impasse that recalls Lamia's confinement, and he even runs the risk of remaining a mere fanatic, as Keats points out in the contemporary incipit of *The Fall of Hyperion*[226]. This emotive tension contributes to the creation of the living symbol. What is now important to consider is the way Lamia breaks this stalemate. Her metamorphosis is produced by Hermes's spell (133: "put to proof the lithe[227] Caducean charm"), and the outcome is a woman who relates to others through magic, more precisely through hypnotic magic. I have

---

[226] *The Fall of Hyperion* begins with the assertion that "Fanatics have their dreams" (1) and that what distinguishes poets from them is precisely "Poesy'"s unique ability to "tell her dreams" (8).

[227] It is noteworthy the recurring of the same adjective that is emphasised in *Hyperion* I 261, where "lithe" underlines the flexibility of the serpent and thus its extraordinary capacity of movement. Here it is not directly referred to the snake Lamia but to the instrument of her metamorphosis, so that her possibility of transformation may be interpreted as a different realisation of the serpent's flexibility and intrinsic dynamism.

already quoted the passages where she entices Lycius through the mesmeric power of her eyes (292-295) and, above all, through her charming singing (249-250, 268-270, 296-299, 322-323). Magic and hypnotism, as seen, symbolise some qualities of poetry according to Romantic principles – precisely the way the insight can be conveyed to the reader through sympathy. As a matter of fact, to arouse empathy is the function of Lamia's voice even when she first appears in the poem, since it is such as to destroy "once heard, in gentle heart [...] / All pain but pity" (36-37).

A serpent endowed with speech and, what is more, with a musical voice is extremely unnatural and conforms to the Romantic conception of creativity, as it represents an insight that is spontaneously conveyed to the reader. It is, in fact, a serpent who has acquired some of the characteristics of the bird. It would seem that we have returned to the perspective of *Endymion*, where the non-Romantic problem of verbalisation is acknowledged but resolved in Romantic terms. However, almost two years had passed and Keats's conception of creativity had considerably developed. It is true that he restates Romantic positions when explaining why he abandoned *Hyperion* and that, in the prologue of *The Fall of Hyperion*, where he deals more explicitly with the poetic communication of the insight, he resorts to magic and identifies "the fine spell of words" (9) as the way of conveying the contents of imagination, that is, in a Romantic unmediated way[228]. Yet Lamia is always twofold. Alongside her magic, musical, womanly powers, she still presents a strong leftover of animality, which manifests itself in the sibilant aspect of her pronunciation and in her desultory lack of empathy[229].

The Romantic model is, actually, further questioned and complicated in the second part of the poem. The technique Keats uses is similar to that of *Endymion*: a same issue is refracted in different passages of the same text and confronted from slightly different perspectives. The beginning of the end starts with "a thrill / Of trumpets" (*Lamia* II 27-28), whose sound leaves "a thought a-buzzing" (29) in Lycius's head. For the first time since he met Lamia, he turns his spirit to "the noisy world almost forsworn" (33), that is, to the world of men. It becomes, indeed, clear that Lamia's transfer from the Other World to the human one has not been completely achieved, since she is confined to a sort of limbo in her "purple-linèd palace of sweet sin" (31). It is interesting that also the colour of the place signifies its liminality, being halfway between the blue of remote

---

228 It is, however, significant that the spell of words is said to save imagination "from the sable charm / And dumb enchantment" (10-11). It has already been underlined how "dumb" suggests an inability to speak, but the other adjective is interesting too, since "sable" is then referred to the trees (446), "Whose arms spread straggling in wild serpent forms" (447). Thus, a further proof of the association between the serpent and the difficulty of expression that risks to entrap imagination may be detected.

229 See the lines 290-291, where she denies Lycius her sympathy.

otherness and the red of approached humanity. Lamia detects "a want / Of something more" (35-36) in Lycius, but what he really wants is her complete integration into the world of men, which is possible only through the acknowledgement of others. Lycius expresses his desire in the following terms:

> What mortal hath a prize, that other men
> May be confounded and abashed withal,
> But lets it something pace abroad majestical,
> And triumph, as in thee I should rejoice
> Amid the hoarse alarm of Corinth's voice. (57-61)

Lycius wants to make his experience of Lamia intersubjective through the institution of marriage, that is, by bringing it from a private dimension to a public one. The isotopy of the latter, in fact, dominates the whole passage, including the opening image of the trumpet, which is usually played in official contexts. If the metapoetic level is taken into account, the public dimension easily corresponds to the dimension of the public. Just as Lycius's relationship with Lamia has value in the human world only if it is sanctioned by other men, so the poet's vision needs a public in order to be communicated and to bring the process of poetic verbalisation to a conclusion. Lycius uses the verb "labyrinth" (53) to indicate the final act of Lamia's insertion in the world of men; as already seen, according to Keats, the maze is a metaphor of the process of poetic composition. In addition, the urge to convey his imaginative insights to the readers usually arises in the poet together with the thought of fame, and, indeed, the official trumpet, the "prize" (57), and the "triumph" (60) are all elements that lead to the isotopy of public celebration, which, in the literary world, corresponds to the notion of fame.

Therefore, Lamia can actually belong to the world of men – and the poetic vision be truly communicated – only if she is acknowledged by them and renounces to be a snake. In fact, as soon as she consents to marry Lycius, she is proclaimed not to be serpent[230]. Lamia's public acknowledgement appears to be inconsistent with her serpent nature, and, indeed, Lycius imposes it upon her as an act of violence[231]. The incompatibility between Lamia's essence – in particular, her serpentine part, which symbolises the unconscious, divergent quality of the insight – and the logic of the society of men parallels the gap between the Other World and the human one that had to be overcome in her previous transformation. Yet the focus has been shifted, since now the central issue revolves, for the first time, around the double notion of public. The main question does not deal simply with turning the vision into words, but with communi-

---

230 "The serpent – ha, the serpent! Certes, she / Was none" (80-81).
231 "He thereat was stung, / Perverse, with stronger fancy to reclaim / Her wild and timid nature to his aim" (69-71).

cating it to the readers. Both processes, however, turn out to be extremely painful for Lamia[232], as they respond to laws that differ from those of her nature.

Lycius's idea of making Lamia known to the people of Corinth is presented as the result of convergent thinking: the sound of the trumpet produces the lingering of a "thought" (29) in Lycius's mind, and Lamia asks him: "Why do you think?" (41) in order to define the activity through which he is distancing himself from her. As already pointed out, Keats usually identifies 'thought' with a conscious, rational, discursive mental activity. This accounts for the incompatibility between Lamia and marriage, that is, between the insight and its intersubjective communication, which is necessary to achieve fame. As language itself responds to asymmetrical laws, its convergent nature is further stressed by its communicative aim, since imposing an order on the divergent contents of imagination by means of intersubjective conventions is especially required to make them intelligible to someone else[233]. The predominance of an asymmetrical mode is also rendered through the concentration of linking words in Lycius's speech, as they indicate a logic or temporal sequence of elements that could not exist in the symmetrical mode[234]. It is thus clear that this attempt to socialise Lycius's union with Lamia – and, on a metapoetic level, the experience of the imaginative insight – does not conform to the Romantic principles, as it is painful and strenuous instead of spontaneous and sympathetic, and relies on convergent means rather than divergent ones. Keats suggests this incompatibility from the outset of the scene, since the "thrill / Of trumpets" (27–28) deafens "the swallow's twitter" (27), i.e. the spontaneous singing of the Romantic bird.

The difficulty of Lamia's integration into the world of men is eventually proven by the failure of Lycius's plan. The nuptial feast, i. e. the most social of the occasions, ends, in fact, with her disappearance. The nature of her vanishing is revealed by what Lamia leaves behind. The last scene parallels her previous metamorphosis into a woman, whose accomplishment is represented through the fact that Lamia melts into the air and only her new musical voice remains lingering. I have interpreted it as an entrance into the dimension of human musicality as well as poetry. At the end of the poem, this dynamics seems to be

---

232 "The lady's cheek / Trembled; she nothing said, but, pale and meek, / Arose and knelt before him, wept a rain / Of sorrows at his words; at last with pain / Beseeching him, the while her hand she wrung, / To change his purpose" (64–69).

233 Even though language intrinsically has a convergent nature, it can be pushed towards its divergent limit in order to represent as faithful as possible the writer's vision, as in the most extreme forms of visionary authors. The outcome, however, is often hardly intelligible.

234 See "Why" (49), "While" (50), "How" (52), "What", "that" (57), "But" (59), "as" (60), "While" (63). It is noteworthy that most of them are found at the beginning of lines, that is, in a position of emphasis and as to articulate the progression of his thought.

reversed. Lamia suddenly disappears, but what remains of her is "a frightful scream" (306), that is, a noise more than a sound. At the same time, the magic music that had been produced by Lamia's spell ceases too[235]. Therefore, Lamia's story ends with a return to the inarticulate, with a shriek substituting enticing singing. In addition, these lines are marked by a concentration of voiceless fricatives, especially sibilants, which suggest a parallel return to the animal dimension of the serpent[236].

The fundamental incompatibility between Lamia and the laws of human society seems to be restated as Lycius's attempt to make his love for Lamia intersubjectively acknowledged fails, but Lamia's disappearance directly depends on a different cause. Lamia vanishes after Apollonius calls her a serpent (305). The word 'serpent' itself, which he pronounces, begins with a continuous sibilant and ends with a plosive, as if to represent the severing action of Apollonius's intervention on Lamia's existence. The same dynamics is repeated in the whole line, which ends with the final plosive of "said" (305), and at the end of the following line in "vanished" (306), where the [t] blocks the [ʃ] and Lamia definitely disappears. Lamia vanishes because of Apollonius's act that is an act of definition[237]: he wants to say what Lamia is and to trap her in the limitations of discriminating, convergent language, an operation which has been shown to be impossible since her very first description. Lamia is not simply a snake: she is a hybrid, she is more colourful and richly adorned than language can tell[238]. As a result, Apollonius's attempt to define Lamia is reductive and hence destructive. It is in this frame of reference that the narrator's comment on philosophy has to be interpreted. Immediately before the final catastrophe, he rhetorically asks: "Do not all charms fly / At the mere touch of cold philosophy?" (645), and adduces the rainbow as an example: "There was an awful rainbow once in heaven: / We know her woof, her texture; she is given / In the dull catalogue of common things" (231-233). The analogy between the rainbow and Lamia is evident since she is said to be "rainbow-sided" (I 54) and "of heavenly progeny"

---

235 See in line 263: "the stately music no more breathes".
236 Fricatives are underlined in the following lines: "'A serpent!' echoed he; no sooner said, / Than with a frightful scream she vanished" (305-306).
237 In Sartre's terms, it can be considered an act of the thetic consciousness, i.e. a positional consciousness that deliberately reflects on its acts while being directed to an outer object (xi-xii, 11-14, 801). The opposition between thetic and non-thetic consciousness is further developed in terms of willed consciousness and spontaneous one (609). Apollonius's act is not an intuitive grasp of Lamia's nature but a deliberate, reflective mental action toward an object, in this case Lamia, which is aware of itself and its consequences.
238 Clarke considers Apollonius's act in a similar way, even though in a different interpretative frame and without pointing out the specific role of convergent language: "if Lamia is not or not only a serpent, then Apollonius' curse may be considered a dispossessive metaphor initiating a reverse metamorphosis" (564).

(II 87). Moreover, the rainbow can be listed in a catalogue after it is reduced to a mere noun, like Lamia at the end of the narration, and this reduction depends on the rational, analytical nature of philosophy, which works "by rule and line" (235) and cannot include the inexhaustible richness of the rainbow.

However, Keats's relationship with philosophy around the period of the composition of *Lamia*, that is, between 28 June 1819 and 5 September 1819, was rather ambiguous. In a letter to Miss Jeffery dated on 9 June 1819, he hoped he had become "a little more of a Philosopher than I was, consequently a little less of a versifying Pet-lamb" (*Letters*, vol. 2, 116), as if philosophy could profit poetic composition. On 5 or 6 August, he wrote to Fanny Brawne: "I am convinced more and more every day that (excepting the human friend Philosopher) a fine writer is the most genuine Being in the World" (*Letters*, vol. 2, 139), where philosophy is even placed above poetry. Philosophy implies a knowledge of the human heart that is useful to the new kind of poetry Keats aims to write[239], but it works through laws that are opposite to those of imagination, or rather to the Romantic model of it, thus it cannot but be problematic.

In spite of the narrator's comment, the relationship between poetry and philosophy is not at the centre of *Lamia*, and the latter is present due to its convergent nature, like a sidelong instance of the wider problem around the possibility to impose convergent restraints on divergent insights. *Lamia* can be read as a representation of the attempt to turn the imaginative insight into words and, what is more, convey it to the reader, an act whose centrality in the creation of poetry is acknowledged by Keats in the almost contemporary incipit of *The Fall of Hyperion*. *Lamia* somehow shows the failure of this attempt, but its focus is, above all, on the set of problems raised by it and left unresolved thanks to the insuppressible ambivalence of the poem's lead character. Hence the interpretative uncertainty around the actual meaning of the story, which, however, should not be found but in this same ambiguity.

On one hand, Lamia conforms to the Romantic conception of creativity as far as her hypnotism and magic are concerned. She relates with Lycius on an empathic level and she possesses the spontaneity of singing that is typical of Romantic birds. She seems to symbolise the insight that mesmerises the poet's consciousness as well as the reader, and the problem of its outer realisation seems to be resolved through the acquisition of sympathetic ability, the scarlet of her approach to humanity. However, the Romantic idea of an unmediated communication is evoked to be found wanting. Lamia's metamorphosis into woman is not effortless at all but, on the contrary, extremely painful, as she needs to overcome the gap between two ontologically different dimensions. Her

---

239 Lamia cannot be accused of the "inexperience of live [*for* life], and simplicity of knowledge" (*Letters*, vol. 2, 174) that distinguishes *Isabella*.

richness has to be filtered – and inevitably restrained – by language in order to fit in our world. Hence the recurring elements of suffering, suffocation and intricacy. Verbalisation affects the poet's vision as an act of violence, since it imposes its own convergent principles on the divergent nature of the other.

After the purely Romantic experience of the odes, Keats had returned to the non-Romantic genre of the narrative poem and even resorted to stylistic devices that belonged to the Augustan art[240], or, as already mentioned, to the Miltonic inversions he had rejected after *Hyperion*. An instance of this stylistic development is the return to the heroic couplet of *Endymion* but with a new attention to the integrity of the line, so that the result is most "closely akin to the Augustan couplet" (Bate 170). Thus, it is not by chance that the former characteristics of the serpent – magic and hypnotism – derive from the Romantic model of Coleridge, while the latter – suffering, suffocation and intricacy – from the non-Romantic Milton. However, it should be borne in mind that this evolution does not mean that Keats embraced an Augustan conception of creativity, since all the questions that are here addressed still revolve around imagination and its contents. The centrality of the imaginative insight in the poetic creation is not questioned, but it is the way of conveying it that poses problems and does so in conjunction with the appearance of the serpent.

Therefore, the Romantic solutions of *Endymion* and the necessary as well as risky constraints of *Hyperion* are both evoked in *Lamia:* they coexist, but are not resolved in a synthesis. The two natures of Lamia as well as the two worlds they stand for continue to be in tension throughout the story as it is typical of a 'living symbol'. The problem of the public – which is actually the driving force of the symbol, since the need to verbalise the insight depends on the poet's need to transform his experience into something that can be read by others – arises in this context and shares the same ambivalence as the rest of the poem. Lamia, in fact, does not truly exist in the world of men until she is acknowledged by them, but, at the same time, this process leads to her destruction. *Lamia* itself is a poem that Keats actually thought in relation to a public[241] and constituted his last attempt to become a poet by profession. On 11 July 1819, he informed Reynolds that he had finished the first part of *Lamia* and commented: "I have great hopes of success, because I make use of my Judgement more deliberately than I yet have

---

240 See Bate 146–171, where he also stresses the stylistic influence of Augustan writers, such as Dryden and Sandys.
241 See the letter to George and Georgiana dated 18 September 1819: "I have been reading over a part of a short poem I have composed lately, called Lamia, and I am certain there is that sort of fire in it that must take hold of people some way. Give them either pleasant or unpleasant sensation – what they want is a sensation of some sort" (*Letters*, vol. 2, 189). He is even more explicit a few days later in a letter to Woodhouse where he expressed his intention to "use more finesse with the Public" (*Letters*, vol. 2, 174).

done; but in Case of failure with the world, I shall find my content" (*Letters*, vol. 2, 128). That success implies an acknowledgement from the reading public is confirmed by the reference to the world, while it is also noteworthy that achievement is linked with the use of the deliberate, rational faculty of judgement, as it is suggested by Lycius's speech. Nevertheless, in the letter to Miss Jeffrey which preceded the beginning of *Lamia*'s composition, Keats confessed an "abatement of my love of fame" (*Letters*, vol. 2, 116).

His relationship with the public had always been contradictory, but it became particularly problematic while he was writing *Lamia*, as shown by the letter he wrote to Reynolds on 24 August 1819: "The more I know what my diligence may in time probably effect; the more does my heart distend with Pride and Obstinacy – I feel it in my power to become a popular writer – I feel it in my strength to refuse the poisonous suffrage of a public" (*Letters*, vol. 2, 146). Keats confessed a certain fascination with the idea of becoming a popular writer, but he was aware of the negative effect the influence of the public can have on an artist. The cost of public acknowledgement is shown in *Lamia* to be probably too high, yet the need for it cannot be entirely avoided. This letter is illustrative of the frame of thought in which *Lamia* was written. The mention of diligence points out the importance Keats had been giving to the convergent aspects[242] of the creative act even after the experience of their excesses in *Hyperion*.

In September 1819, he wrote to George and Georgiana: "Some think I have lost that poetic ardour and fire 't is said I once had – the fact is perhaps I have: but instead of that I hope I shall substitute a more thoughtful and quiet power" (*Letters*, vol. 2, 209). Keats seems definitely directed towards a more constrained, controlled way of writing, which, however, does not betray the fundamental Romantic lesson. As a matter of fact, the letters analysed above, where he restates his Romantic belief in relation to the failed experiment of *Hyperion*, date back to this same month, and the letter to Reynolds ends with Keats's Romantic assertion that he is in a "state of excitement" where he cannot say "but what I feel" and which is "the only state for the best sort of Poetry" (*Letters*, vol. 2, 147). Excitement alternates with thoughtfulness as Keats seems to be striving towards a personal way of resolving some of the crucial Romantic issues. Yet the tragic ending of *Lamia* leaves the problem unresolved: the attempt to include the serpent in our world is unsuccessful. It vanishes and eludes us once again.

---

242 In the letter to Miss Jeffery, he wrote: "I dare say my discipline is to come, and plenty of it too" (*Letters*, vol. 2, 116).

Conclusion

The serpent has been shown to be an extremely significant as well as productive symbol for Keats. It remains active throughout almost the entirety of his poetic career, and turns out to be particularly suitable for conveying some of the most important and problematic issues of his reflections about creativity in the form of powerful images. In particular, the 'living symbol' of the snake was generated by Keats out of the tension between the Romantic view of the poetic act, which almost exclusively favours its unconscious, divergent dimension, and the need to resort to some of the convergent, deliberate aspects that the Romantics rejected as belonging to the Augustan view of art. Keats felt all this tension, as he agreed with the Romantics in placing imagination at the centre of the poetic creation but, at the same time, gradually became aware that the spontaneous arousal of the imagination is not sufficient to write a poem, since the poet's symmetrical insight needs to pass through some asymmetrical filter – be it narrative structure or language itself – in order to become intelligible and communicable to the reader.

If it is true that at the beginning of his career Keats had violently rejected the Augustan idea of poetic craftsmanship in favour of the Romantic view, which he had to endorse or at least to confront to be acknowledged as a poet in those years, it has been seen that he gradually revaluated the role of discipline and judgement in composition, and even pointed out the need to restrain imagination, although the latter always remained the chief poetic faculty. The serpent appears precisely at those moments when the Romantic paradigm of spontaneous communication of the imaginative insight, which is perfectly embodied by the instinctive singing of birds, is called into question. Thanks to some of its characteristics – such as the unexpectedness of its appearances as well as disappearances, its intricate form and its hypnotic eyes –, the snake most appropriately conveys the sudden emergence into consciousness of an imaginative content. Yet Keats's serpents are almost always in pain, they writhe and convulse, but, most importantly, they are somewhat affected by suffocation, that is, by a difficulty in emitting sound which corresponds to a difficulty of expression and is already implied in their dysphoric, inarticulate hissing. Thus, the serpent often captures the moment when the insight manifests itself to consciousness but has to struggle in order to be verbalised and turned into actual poetry.

It has been said that the hindrance to an unmediated, effortless communication of the poet's divergent vision depends on the need to submit it to convergent processes, which correspond, first of all, to the act of verbalisation itself, but not exclusively. In fact, if the symbol of the serpent always works within this paradigm, it should not be forgotten that living symbols are insuppressibly dynamic, so that the snake comes to represent different specific problems inside this general frame of reference in every different poem, but also in a single composition. Therefore, the serpent cannot be said to stand for imagination or verbalisation, since it is generated by a tension that continuously shifts the precise terms of its opposition. This is the reason why the serpent continuously changes its meaning throughout Keats's poetic production, and focusing on its symbolism has allowed us to follow the development of Keats's conception of imagination as well as the problem of the poetic communication of its contents. I have started with the episode of Glaucus in Book 3 of *Endymion*, where the appearance of snakes raises the issue, which, nonetheless, is resolved in accordance with the Romantic principles. Even though, in this period, Keats still completely adhered to the Romantic idea of poetic composition as a spontaneous, inspired act, represented in the form of mesmeric or musical magic, he chose to write his first important poetic achievement as a long narrative poem, a genre that was not typically Romantic and that presented him with the need to resort to a convergent faculty such as invention.

The symbol of the serpent, which is, indeed, far more frequent in narrative poems, is generated out of this contradiction, but in *Hyperion* the main focus shifts to another issue. The serpent, which appears here in all its suffocating quality as a simile for agony, represents the imposition of a disciplined style that is modelled after Milton on the contents of imagination and the moment when this new restraint risks becoming too inhibiting, as proven by the incompleteness of the poem, which Keats justifies through a return to Romantic assertions. Lastly, *Lamia* offers the depiction of a highly unusual snake that is endowed with a heavenly voice, creating a parallel with the Romantic bird, and which is actually not even entirely a snake, but rather a hybrid creature. The twofoldness of her nature – serpent and woman – reflects the two worlds across which her metamorphosis makes her move. *Lamia* can be seen as a symbol of the failed attempt to turn the imaginative insight into language and to make it intersubjectively communicable just as Lamia fails to integrate entirely into the world of men. Keats approaches here the problem from both Romantic and non-Romantic perspectives without, however, resolving their tension in a synthesis. What is more innovative compared to his previous works is the emphasis on the public, since Lamia's integration into the world of men can be achieved only through a public acknowledgement that leads, instead, to her disappearance. Keats gives voice here to his own ambivalent attitude towards fame, since *Lamia* itself is conceived as his last attempt to become a popular writer but also contains the awareness that this may have an excessive cost at the expense of the authenticity of imagination.

The present study has, therefore, attempted to point out the crucial role that serpent symbolism plays in giving shape in poetry to a set of interrelated problems that concern the creative process, and are an important matter of concern to Keats and one to which he constantly returns in his letters. I have limited my analysis to the snake because its relevance to Keats's entire production has so far failed to get due critical attention, but it would be interesting to extend the study first of all to the other reptiles that are present, even if far less frequently, in Keats's poetry – such as crocodiles[243] and dragons[244] – in order to see how their representation differs from that of snakes and how their peculiarities affect their possible metapoetic interpretation. At the same time, bird symbolism would be worthy of a thorough survey as well. I have been compelled by the length and complexity of the topic to limit it to a few observations about the opposition between birds and snakes, but the metapoetic elements of bird symbolism would undoubtedly deserve a more in-depth study, as birds are the animals that recur most often in Keats's whole poetic production. Ultimately, Keats's overall animal symbolism may be interestingly analysed by taking an approach that takes into consideration the relationship that different animals may have with different aspects of Keats's conception of creativity, so as to reveal new aspects of his relationship with his own creative process as well as the way his concerns about it are transferred into his poetic practice.

---

243 See *Endymion* I 714, IV 245 and "To the Nile" 2.
244 See "To Mary Frogley" 64, "Upon my life, Sir Nevis, I am piqued" 55, 59 and 60, *The Eve of St. Agnes* 353 and *Otho the Great* II ii 64.

Bibliography

Primary sources

Burton, Robert. *The Anatomy of Melancholy*. Edited by T.C. Faulkner, N.K. Kiessling e R.L. Blair, Clarendon, [1621] 1990-1992. 3 vols.
Coleridge, Samuel T. *Poetical Works*. Edited by Ernest Hartley Coleridge, Oxford University Press, [1912] 1967.
–. *Biographia Literaria, or, Biographical Sketches of My Literary Life and Opinions*. Edited with his aesthetical essays by John Shawcross, Oxford University Press, [1817] 1967.
–. *Lectures 1808-1819: On the History of Philosophy*. Edited by Earl Leslie Griggs, vol. 1, Princeton University Press, 2000.
Keats, John. *The Complete Poems*. Edited by Miriam Allott, Longman, [1970] 1986.
–. *The Letters of John Keats: 1814-1821*. Edited by H.E. Rollins, Harvard University Press, 1958. 2 vols.
The Holy Bible, Containing the Old and New Testaments: Translated out of the Original Tongues and with the Former Translations Diligently Compared and Revised by His Majesty's Special Command. Appointed to be Read in Churches. Authorised King James Edition. Collins' Clear-Type Press, 1958.
Lemprière, John. *Classical Dictionary of Proper Names Mentioned in Ancient Authors*. Routledge & Kegan Paul, [1788] 1951.
Milton, John. *Paradise Lost*. Edited by Christopher Ricks, Penguin Books, [1667] 1989.
Ovid. *Metamorphoses*. Edited with an introduction, translation and notes by D.E. Hill, Aris & Phillips, 1999.
Philostratus. *The Life of Apollonius of Tyana*. Edited and translated by Christopher P. Jones, vol. 1, Harvard University Press, 2005.
Rollins, Hyder E., editor. *The Keats Circle: Letters and Papers and More Letters and Poems of the Keats Circle*. 2nd ed., Harvard University Press, 1965. 2 vols.
Sandys, George. *Ovid's Metamorphosis*. Edited by Daniel Kinney, University of Virginia, [1623]: http://ovid.lib.virginia.edu/sandys/contents.htm.
Shakespeare, William. *The Poems*. Edited by F.T. Prince, Harvard University Press, 1961.
Shelley, Mary. *Frankenstein, or, The Modern Prometheus*. Edited with an Introduction by M.K. Joseph, Oxford University Press, [1818] 1971.
Shelley, Percy B. *Shelley's Poetry and Prose*. Selected and edited by Donald H. Reiman and Neil Fraistat, 2nd ed., W.W. Norton, 2002.

Swift, Jonathan. *A Tale of a Tub: To which is added The Battle of the Books and the Mechanical Operation of the Spirit.* Edited by A.C. Guthkelch and D. Nichol Smith, Clarendon Press, [1704] 1958.

Virgil. *The Eclogues and Georgics.* Edited with introduction and notes by R.D. Williams, St. Martin Press, 1979.

Wordsworth, William. *Poetical Works.* Edited by Thoman Hutchinson and revised by Ernest de Selincourt, Oxford University Press [1950] 1964.

Wordsworth, William, and T. S. Coleridge. *Lyrical Ballads.* Edited by R.L. Brett and A.R. Jones, Methuen, [1798] 1965.

Young, Edward. "Conjectures on Original Composition." *Critical Theory Since Plato*, edited by Hazard Adams and Leroy Searle, 3rd ed., Thomson/Wadsworth, 2005, pp. 348–356.

Secondary sources

Abrams, Meyer H. *The Mirror and the Lamp: Romantic Theory and the Critical Tradition.* Oxford University Press, [1953] 1971.

Attridge, Derek. *Poetic Rhythm: An Introduction.* Cambridge University Press, [1995] 2008.

Aske, Martin. *Keats and Hellenism: An Essay.* Cambridge University Press, 1985.

Bate, Walter J. *The Stylistic Development of Keats.* The Humanities Press, [1945] 1962.

Baumbach, Sibylle. *Literature and Fascination.* Palgrave Macmillan, 2015.

Bostetter, Edward E. "The Eagle and the Truth: Keats and the Problem of Belief." *The Journal of Aesthetics and Art Criticism*, vol. 16, no. 3, 1958, pp. 362–372.

Bush, Douglas. *Mythology and the Romantic Tradition in English Poetry.* Harvard University Press, 1969.

Caldwell, Janis M. *Literature and Medicine in Nineteenth-Century Britain: From Mary Shelley to George Eliot.* Cambridge University Press, 2004.

Chambers, Jane. "'For Love's Sake': *Lamia* and Burton's Melancholy Love." *Studies in English Literature: 1500–1900*, vol. 22, no. 4, 1982, pp. 583–600.

Clarke, Bruce. "Fabulous Monsters of Conscience: Anthropomorphosis in Keats's *Lamia*." *Studies in Romanticism*, vol. 23, no. 4, 1984, pp. 555–579.

Cowden Clarke, Charles and Mary. *Recollections of Writers.* Introduced by Robert Gittings, Centaur Press, 1969.

De Almeida, Hermione. *Romantic Medicine and John Keats.* Oxford University Press, 1991.

DeLong, Anne. *Mesmerism, Medusa, and the Muse: The Romantic Discourse of Spontaneous Creativity.* Lexington Books, 2012.

Doležel, Lubomír. *Occidental Poetics: Tradition and Progress.* University of Nebraska Press, 1990.

Douka-Kabitoglou, Ekaterini. "Adapting Philosophy to Literature: The Case of John Keats." *Studies in Philology*, vol. 89, no. 1, 1992, pp. 115–136.

Durand, Gilbert. *The Anthropological Structures of the Imagery.* Boombana Publications, 1999.

Ford, Newell F. "Keats, Empathy, and 'The Poetical Character'." *Studies in Philology*, vol. 45, no. 3, 1948, pp. 477–490.
Freud, Sigmund. *The Complete Introductory Lectures on Psychoanalysis*. Translated and edited by James Strachey, W.W. Norton, 1966.
Goellnicht, Donald C. *The Poet-Physician: Keats and Medical Science*. University of Pittsburgh Press, 1984.
Hannah, Barbara. *The Archetypal Symbolism of Animals: Lectures Given at the C.G. Jung Institute, Zurich, 1954–1958*. Edited by David Eldred. Chiron Publications, 2006.
Heymans, Peter. *Animality in British Romanticism: The Aesthetics of Species*. Routledge, 2012.
Hill, John S. (ed.). *Keats: Narrative Poems*. Macmillan, 1983.
Horne, Jackie C. *History and the Construction of the Child in Early British Children's Literature*. Routledge, [2011] 2016.
Hrushovski, Benjamin. "The Meaning of Sound Patters in Poetry: An Interaction Theory." *Poetics Today*, vol. 2, no. 1a, 1980, pp. 39–56.
Jacobs, Vivian and Wilhelmina. "The Color Blue: Its Use as Metaphor and Symbol". *American Speech*, vol. 3, no. 1, 1958, pp. 29–46.
Jung, Carl J. *Symbols of Transformation* (*Collected Works*, vol. 5). A Revision by R.F.C. Hull of the translation by H.G. Baynes. 2nd ed., Princeton University Press, [1912] 1967.
–. *Psychological Types* (*Collected Works*, vol. 6). A Revision by R.F.C. Hull of the translation by H.G. Baynes. 2nd ed., Princeton University Press, [1921] 1976.
–. *Psychology and Alchemy* (*Collected Works*, vol. 12). A Revision by R.F.C. Hull of the translation by H.G. Baynes. 2nd ed., Princeton University Press, [1944] 1968.
–. *Aion: Researches into the Phenomenology of the Self* (*Collected Works*, vol. 9.II). A Revision by R.F.C. Hull of the translation by H.G. Baynes. 2nd ed., Princeton University Press, [1951] 1979.
–. *Two Essays in Analytical Psychology* (*Collected Works*, vol. 7). A Revision by R.F.C. Hull of the translation by H.G. Baynes. 2nd ed., Princeton University Press, [1952] 1966.
–. *The Archetypes and the Collective Unconscious* (*Collected Works*, vol. 9.I). A Revision by R.F.C. Hull of the translation by H.G. Baynes. 2nd ed., Princeton University Press, [1933–1954] 1968.
–. *Alchemical Studies* (*Collected Works*, vol. 13). A Revision by R.F.C. Hull of the translation by H.G. Baynes. 2nd ed., Princeton University Press, [1942–1957] 1967.
–. *Psychogenesis of Mental Disease* (*Collected Works*, vol. 3). A Revision by R.F.C. Hull of the translation by H.G. Baynes. 2nd ed., Princeton University Press, [1907–1958] 1982.
–. *Children's Dreams: Notes from the Seminar Given in 1936–1940*. Edited by Lorenz Jung and Maria Meyer-Grass and translated by Ernst Falzeder. Princeton University Press, [1987] 2008.
Kenyon-Jones, Christine. *Kindred Brutes: Approaches to Animals in Romantic-Period Writing, with Special Reference to Byron*. Dissertation, King's College London, 1999. UMI, 2001.
Lau, Beth. *Keats's Paradise Lost*. University Press of Florida, 1998.
Li, Ou. *Keats and Negative Capability*. Bloomsbury Academic, 2009.
Lobis, Seth. *The Virtue of Sympathy: Magic, Philosophy, and Literature in Seventeenth-Century England*. Yale University Press, 2015.

Matte Blanco, Ignacio. *The Unconscious as Infinite Sets: An Essay in Bi-Logic.* Duckworth, 1975.

Murry, John Middleton. *Keats and Shakespeare: A Study of Keats' Poetic Life from 1816 to 1820.* Oxford University Press, [1925] 1949.

O'Neill, Michael. "*Lamia:* 'Things Real – Things Semireal – and No Things'." *The Challenge of Keats. Bicentenary Essays 1795–1995*, edited by Allan C. Christensen, Lilla Maria Crisafulli Jones, Giuseppe Galigani and Anthony J. Johnson, Rodopi, 2000.

Owings, Frank N. *The Keats Library: (a descriptive catalogue).* Keats-Shelley Memorial Association, 1978.

Patterson, Charles I. *The Daemonic in the Poetry of John Keats.* University of Illinois Press, 1970.

Pedrini, Lura N. and Duilio T. *Serpent Imagery and Symbolism: A Study of the Major English Romantic Poets.* College and University Press, 1966.

Perkins, David. *Romanticism and Animal Rights.* Cambridge University Press, 2003.

Pope, Rob. *Creativity: Theory, History, Practice.* Routledge, 2005.

Radden, Jennifer, editor. *The Nature of Melancholy: from Aristotle to Kristeva.* Oxford University Press, 2000.

Ridley, Maurice R. *Keats's Craftsmanship: A Study in Poetic Development.* Russel & Russel, [1933] 1962.

Routh, James. "Parallels in Coleridge, Keats, and Rossetti." *Modern Language Notes*, vol. 25, no. 2, 1910, pp. 33–37.

Sallis, John. *Force of imagination: The Sense of the Elemental.* Indiana University Press, 2000.

Sartre, Jean-Paul. *Being and Nothingness: A Phenomenological Essay on Ontology.* Translated and with an Introduction by Hazel E. Barnes, Washington Square Press, [1943] 1956.

Sawyer, R. Keith. *Explaining Creativity: The Science of Human Innovation.* Oxford University Press, 2006.

Seright, Orin D. *Syntactic Structures in Keats' Poetry.* Indiana University, 1964.

Sinson, Janice C. *John Keats and the Anatomy of Melancholy.* Keats-Shelley Memorial Association, 1971.

Stillinger, Jack. *Romantic Complexity: Keats, Coleridge, and Wordsworth.* University of Illinois Press, 2006.

Slote, Bernice. *Keats and the Dramatic Principle.* Nebraska University Press, 1958.

Stewart, Garrett. "*Lamia* and the Language of Metamorphosis." *Studies in Romanticism*, vol. 15, no. 1, 1976, pp. 3–41.

Swaim, Kathleen M. "The Art of the Maze in Book IX of *Paradise Lost*". *Studies in English Literature, 1500–1900*, vol. 12, no. 1, 1972, pp. 129–140.

Tsur, Reuven. *What Makes Sound Patterns Expressive?: The Poetic Mode of Speech Perception.* Duke University Press, 1992.

Ward, Aileen. "Keats and Burton: A Reappraisal." *Philological Quarterly*, vol. 40, no. 4, 1961, pp. 535–552.

Zimmerman, Sarah M. *Romanticism, Lyricism, and History.* State University of New York Press, 1999.